The Whale Whisperer

The Whale Whisperer

Healing Messages from the Animal Kingdom
to help Mankind and the Planet

Madeleine Walker

FINDHORN PRESS

Findhorn Press
One Park Street
Rochester, Vermont 05767
www.findhornpress.com

Findhorn Press is a division of Inner Traditions International

ISBN 978-1-84409-537-7

Cataloging-in-Publication Data for this title is available from the British Library

Printed and bound in the United States

Edited and typeset by Maggie Aldred
Cover design by Damian Keenan
Cover photograph by Urs Buehler

Photography;
Urs Buehler pp. 97, 98, 103, Karen-Jane Dudley pp. 159, 163,
James Edwards pp. 129, Jacqueline Russell pp. 143,
Jason Turner pp. 197, Alexander Turoff pp. 83, 86, 107

"Our journey is long and dangerous, especially for our little ones. We sing our song of love for mother Gaia. We sing our song to bring balance to ourselves and the earth. Mankind has brought discordance and death to so many of us over time, but we still choose to bring healing and the recognition of the need to love all creation. All is divine and contains divinity within. The echoes of our song's vibrations resonate that message through each water molecule of the sea that splashes and sprays this message onto the rocks and shores, infusing the land with our song's energy and clarion call to all."
—The Southern Right Whales, Hermanus, South Africa, October 2009

"We as humans have to let go of feelings of separation and reclaim our sense of self, to remember that there is only love. That is the animals' gift. They open us up to communication with them, so that we can communicate with ourselves. We have drifted so far from our truth, the animals are here to gently nudge us back. on our path of understanding."
—Excerpt from *An Exchange of Love* by Madeleine Walker

"What is man without the beasts? If all the beasts were gone, man would die from a great loneliness of spirit. For whatever happens to the beasts, soon happens to man. All things are connected."
—Chief Dan George

"The greatness of a nation and its moral progress can be judged by the way its animals are treated."
—Mahatma Gandhi

"Our lives begin to end the day we become silent about things that matter."
—Martin Luther King Jnr.

"The great use of life is to spend it for something that will outlast it."
(—W. James)

For my wonderful mother Rosalinde.

Her grace and courage in the face of
adversity is a constant inspiration to me.

Mere words cannot express my
gratitude or love for her.

*"We speak of mysteries in our squawks and magic
in our chatters. If you would but slow to
nature's ebb and flow, you would hear what
really matters!"*

—Message from the ravens

CONTENTS

CONTENTS

FOREWORD

Today, animal communication is the most powerful tool we humans possess to re-establish a loving and meaningful relationship with the real world. Although this ability dates back to ancient times, it is critically relevant to our modern day, and is *the key* not only to protecting our planet but also to saving ourselves. That's why Madeleine Walker's inspiring book *The Whale Whisperer* is so important, and so timeous.

I speak from personal experience, since the incident that saved my own life took place in a wilderness area in South Africa's bushveld region known as Timbavati, when I was rescued from a pride of angry lions by an indigenous medicine woman, who communicated with the king of the beasts, and asked for safe passage. Lions are nocturnal predators, but this amazing woman walked on foot, at night, with her grandchild on her back, through a pride of some 24 lions who had been snarling aggressively moments before. She calmed them, and came to my rescue. How? By speaking to the lions as if they were her family, which she truly believed these majestic animals to be. The lions were angry, and they had reason to be. For years humans had been hunting the rare White Lions of that region to the brink of extinction.

This near-death experience changed my life. I gave up my hectic job in advertizing and marketing, and returned to Africa to find this woman. I discovered that she was known as Maria Khosa, Lion Queen of Timbavati, and that she originated from an ancient lineage of animal communicators. She became my teacher, and what she had to teach was more important than anything I had learned in the hallowed halls of Cambridge University. She showed me there are only two simple rules to working with Mother Nature: *Love* and *Respect*. If you follow these you will never be harmed, and Nature herself will protect you.

You will see these two simple principles in all Madeleine's interactions with animals. That's what makes her such a superb communicator. And that's what make this book such a delightful read.

In finding our connection with animals, we find ourselves. *That's the key.* Madeleine Walker's book will assist you to apply these timeless principles in everyday life, and also encourage you to immediately take up the challenge of helping to protect our precious Earth.

The wisdom Madeleine transmits, direct from the animals, will encourage you to do so too. In facing up to challenges in your life, and in choosing to make a meaningful difference for our planet, everyone might experience moments of fear or doubt. At such times, you will find strength and courage by calling on your true lion-heart. Mandla, King of Kings, encourages you to do so in the beautiful meditation on 'Finding your lion heart' in the final chapter.

If you find the idea of communicating with a lion daunting, then begin with your domestic pets, but never forget there is a wonderous world of Nature out there with which we can and should connect.

It was a joy to have Madeleine join me in the sacred White Lion territories. Since Maria Khosa's initiation, I have worked with many accomplished animal communicators: Lesley-Temple Thurston, Amelia Kinkade, Wynter Worsthorne, Anna Breytenbach and Pea Horsly. Like Madeleine, they are all walking in the footsteps of my lion-hearted teacher, and they communicate with animals as if these beautiful creatures are part of our own family, because that's truly what they are.

My experience with the lions of Timbavati taught me that we humans are here to nurture and cherish Mother Earth, and I've committed every day of my life since then to make a meaningful difference. Hopefully, each one of you will come to the same realization, without having to go through the terrifying initiation it took for me to wake up!

Enjoy the adventure…

—Linda Tucker, CEO, Global White Lion Protection Trust, author of *Mystery of the White Lions*, Mantel Holder, 'Keeper of the White Lions'

PREFACE

Madeleine Walker has amazed me many times with her courage and downright determination. When you read this book, you too will be amazed, but also amused, as she recounts her exploits and adventures.

I am one of many who believe that the future of this planet depends on how we interact with the other native life on Earth. Too many people regard animals as playthings, to be mistreated, and abused. And yet, we are all connected, and all the harm that we cause to animals will eventually rebound on us. If children were taught to cherish and care for their pets, they would grow up to be far more responsible human beings.

Madeleine is a rare kind of animal communicator. Yes, she talks to domestic pets, and also to gentle horses, but she also talks to animals that have gone 'wrong', whose strength and anger would make the strongest man quake. She also talks to the wild. She's swum and communicated with some of the biggest and most dangerous of the oceans inhabitants. She has also been up close and personal with white lions. All of this is remarkable and as you take this journey with her, like me you'll feel privileged to have joined her on it.

What is almost more incredible is that Madeleine has done all of this alone. Being divorced brings a lot of people to their knees, especially when the breakup happens unexpectedly. Many women embarking on their fifties would be stopped in their tracks at this kind of betrayal, and withdraw into their shells. Instead, Madeleine embarked on a new part of her life, finding out how to travel alone, braving wild places and interacting with indigenous people. There are many animal communication books out there, but this one stands at the pinnacle. It is an example to us all of what can be achieved, and more importantly what must be achieved if human beings are to survive.

—Jenny Smedley, author of *Pets Have Souls Too*

A whale of a tale

This emotive and at times, humorous book, tells the true story of a 50 something divorcee who feels that there has to be more to life. She is compelled to find her reason for being here, and to connect with her spirituality. She learns to cope with grief at the death of her mother and the devastation of divorce, finding meaning in her feelings of abandonment, reframing them into a sense of freedom and expansion. As her awareness grows, she is compelled to journey to many places around the world on her own, communing with wild species and visiting sacred sites. Along the way she finds herself overcoming fears, adversity and challenges. She gets up close and personal with humpback whales, whale sharks, dolphins and manta rays, white buffalo, elephants and lions. She learns to communicate with these wonderful creatures and discovers that there are very profound messages of hope for our future to be learnt from the creatures who are so much more in tune to the Earth's energy than we are.

The following chapters are the chronological journeys that she has experienced and the growing awareness of the importance of the wisdom of the animals. She realizes that she has to convey these messages so that others can listen and learn from their wisdom, joining to create positive change for us and the planet. She is guided by the white lions to be 'lion-hearted' and to take up the challenge to be the 'voice' of the animals. These communications not only give guidance on the importance of the role of animals in the future of the world, they also reassure that however traumatic and confusing life can be, with the help of the animals we are on 'track' on our soul journeys. We are not alone on our quest to find ourselves; the animals are ready, willing and able to bring us back home. In learning to honour ourselves, we honour the planet.

Introduction

"Make sure you do everything you've ever dreamt of before you die, don't put it off and say 'one day'. That one day may never come or it may be the wrong kind of one day and you never know what's around the corner!", my mother emphasized. My mother's 'wrong day' came gently on the 6th of July 2004. She passed with such grace as my brother and I held her hand in silent vigil, wondering how we would cope without her loving presence. She had had many adventures in her life, but she always wished she could have done more. Her amazing courage and dignity in the way she coped with her illness was an inspiration to everyone who was fortunate enough to connect with her.

I remember her words every time I'm lucky enough to embark on a new adventure. I thank her with all my heart, when I'm sitting in some wonderful place celebrating the beauty of the earth. For her small legacy has enabled me to have adventures and expand my being and find my true self at last. I have visited the most amazing places, encountered fabulous creatures, and felt the sacred vibrations of ancient sites around the world. This has allowed me to expand my awareness and intuitive skills, reclaiming and empowering the real me. Since her passing, I realized that she has endowed me with so many gifts, and that her legacy is far more than purely financial. She kindled my love of animals and nature. Our home was always full of a strange assortment of creatures which she always found board, lodgings and love for. I hope to repay her by conveying the vital information and using the gifts I have been given on these momentous adventures. I know that with her guidance, I have utilized my journeys as not just a vacation, but have gleaned powerful messages from the sacred sites and creatures that I have met. This is a book of hope and re-empowerment and when I look back at the small, almost random things that have led me on my journey, I can see that I was being guided. The certainty that this is important, and that I have to experience it in order to further my knowledge or skills, has better equipped me to help the planet and its inhabitants in whatever way is most appropriate. The universe works in mysterious and wonderful ways. When I retraced the steps that led me to my present reality, I realize that my mother's courage has been the driving force behind me and continues to push me forwards. Although I miss her physical presence every day, I know she watches over me, I'm sure sometimes laughing at my deliberations, but always overwhelming me with her love.

> *"The soul is the same thing in all living creatures,*
> *although the body of each is different."*
> —Hippocrates

A cathartic dream

In the dying embers of 2009, I had a dream – another 'lion' dream. I had dreamt about lions all my life and as a young child these dreams terrified me. Often a huge male lion would leap into our midst, somewhere in the house or garden. This would cause chaos and terror to myself and everyone else in my dream. Sometimes the lion would attack me and I would awake screaming before anything awful happened, but I felt the threat of some terrible end. As I grew older the dreams changed in that I would be nurturing the lions by feeding them. Then, after a trip where I lived on the ocean for a week with humpback whales, my lion dreams took on a whole new dimension. I would actually change into a lioness and become one of the pride. These dreams were so vivid, I actually felt like I could shake off the African dust from my skin and that I would be able to pick out thorns from my hide. I would awaken tucked up in my bed feeling very disorientated, and be surprised to see my hands instead of large paws. I met a wonderful therapist who felt that my recurring lion dreams were about my sense of power, and that I had been afraid of my power, but now that I was making my spiritual connections, I was allowing that power to reawaken. When I first met her, I didn't feel like I had any power, but as I worked with her and we discussed how I could reclaim that power, I began to understand a little of rediscovering my soul purpose, and to take up the reins of my spiritual journey. I felt the whales had imbued me with so much strength and awareness, that I was ready to take on much more profound connections with animals. Since then, my life has changed beyond recognition. I have started learning healing modalities and found that I could communicate telepathically with animals. I learnt how incredible our connections are with them and how much they care about our emotional and physical wellbeing. I understand now that some of the stories in my first book, *An Exchange of Love*, have had an even deeper impact on me than I realized, and only now the full meanings of my journeys are evolving, so it is great to expand on them, giving more detail and the wider concepts of why I experienced all that I did back then.

I had another 'scary' dream that I knew was important. I had returned a couple of months previously from visiting the white lions in South Africa, tracking them daily in our jeep. There were two golden lionesses that had been brought into the pride for the two related male white lions to form a new pride, in order to prevent in-breeding. However much we tried to track the lionesses, during my stay, I never saw them, but here in my dream, they were poised ready to attack in my childhood home front garden. I felt they were very hungry and if I didn't find something for them to feed on, they would see me as their next meal. There was also a huge snake in the dream that had blocked my path and I could see that it had just eaten a large mouse and I saw it squirming inside the snake's belly. In my dream state, I started to shout "Linda, Linda". I was calling for Linda Tucker, who was responsible for the release and protection of the white lions in South Africa, but she never came to my rescue. As I looked down the garden path, I was aware that the postman would be coming soon, and I was worried that the lionesses would attack him. I was feeling very fearful as I knew I didn't have enough food to satisfy them and they would probably be coming for me. I awoke on New Year's Day, feeling very anxious, realizing that it was morning and high time I got up, relieved that it was still the school holidays, and that my teenage son would happily remain in bed until much later in the morning. However, I would have to get up and let my dogs out and get them walked. As I was about to get out of bed, I began to feel strangely excited and a sense of huge anticipation of something momentous for 2010. I just knew this was going to be a very special and important year, in preparation for 2012, which has been foretold as a year of planetary change.

I had just finished reading *Summer with Leprechauns* by Tanis Helliwell, which really opened up my awareness to elementals and nature spirits. I had a favourite tree in the woods where I walked and I always felt that if there were fairies in that wood, they would live in and around 'my' tree. I always got the feeling that I could hear their tinkling laughter, if I could only listen really carefully. We arrived at the place where I walked most mornings. On this particular morning, I thought I would ask the elementals to join me on the walk and help me decipher my dream and help me find an outlet for my messages. These messages were from the creatures that I had been communicating with around the world and also some exciting case studies I had been working on. All the messages I had been intuiting were for the betterment of the planet and mankind. I had been trying to get new book proposals accepted by more spiritual publishers, as I felt compelled to try and reach a wider audience for this imperative information. I was 'told' that morning as I marched out with my dogs that I needed to just 'write it' and to not try and dumb it down. I had to 'tell it like it is'! Those who were ready to hear the profound meaning of the messages from the creature sentient beings would hear and absorb them. I thanked the dogs for giving me the incentive, despite the weather, and as I was climbing, I welcomed the nature elementals and inner earth beings that Tanis had talked about in her wonderful book. I thanked them for reinforcing my resolve that these messages are very important and that we have to listen to the wisdom of the animal kingdom if we are to have any future on this planet. They told me to send it to publishers who care about the spiritual aspects of the planet and its inhabitants. They also suggested that I combine the different book ideas I had into one book that described how animals were helping to heal the past, present and the future of mankind and the planet, and for me to describe the information by relaying my journeys, both spiritually and physically. I asked how I could encapsulate all this and what the book should be called. I was instructed, very firmly, that the book should be titled *The Whale Whisperer*. I questioned this as I communicated with many different creatures. However, I was reminded of a conversation I'd had recently, where I was asked what the most profound message I had ever received from a creature had been, and I had to admit it was from the whales, so yes, the title made perfect sense!

The elementals also helped me to interpret my dream. I had attended a dream workshop in the past and we had been taught to look at all the components of the dream. So I reviewed the different parts of the dream as far as I could remember. I thought about the meaning of the snake. I felt that it symbolized transformation, and that the mouse was my fear that had been swallowed. Calling out the name Linda was very interesting, as my first name is Linda, but I never liked it, so I took my second name, Madeleine, after my grandmother. Ironically her maiden name was Walker; it dawned on me one day, after I was married, that I now had her full name. She had died when my mother was young so I never met her, but had always felt a connection to her and it seemed strange that after all these years, I should have both of her names! It was interesting that the Linda 'energy' did not come to my rescue and that I was who I was meant to be. Although I felt in the dream that the snake was blocking my path, I realized that it was forcing me to embrace my changes. Then moving on to the golden lionesses in my childhood garden, I remembered that although I never physically saw them, I had felt their presence, and had been quite unnerved by the stench of a kill they had made in the bush, right next to the track we were on in our jeep.

Their powers of camouflage prevented us spotting them, but their raw energy, emanating from the nearby scrub, brought up quite primordial feelings of fear within me. I had felt no fear with the white lions that I had seen daily, and so I deduced that the reason for my fear in the dream was the unknown and that I needed to conquer any remaining fear about my power. I also mused about the lack of meat that I had to feed them. I thought it might be because I was vegetarian, but maybe it was about having enough personal power to overcome my perceived challenges. Maybe I needed to reflect where I had given my power away in the past? I wondered what the significance of the postman might be and I surmised it might be that I needed to protect any vulnerable aspects of my life. It was a little unclear until I returned home! So much information had come through thick and fast, I suddenly realized I had ascended the hill with no effort whatsoever. I realized that the postman had come in my absence. I found a belated Christmas card from a new friend called Bob. In the card, stuck down with a bit of sellotape, was a beautiful gold coin. On the face of it was a roaring lion's head. He said that he had found the coin during a recent house move and that it had been given to him ages ago, but when he had rediscovered it, he'd thought of me! On the reverse side was an image of an eland. The eland bulls I had met in Africa told me they symbolized personal power. I felt that this was perhaps yet more synchronicity of leonine energy roaring out, once again reconnecting me with my power.

   The more I thought about all the co-incidences and the meaning of the messages of the dream unfolding, and my wonderful revelations on the walk, the more I determined to set down all the guidance that was given to me on my walking meditation. Now was the time to step up to the plate and communicate in a way that could be accepted and assimilated into our consciousness, so that we can truly understand the magic and wisdom of the creature sentient beings on our beautiful planet.

Horse healers: healing the past to prepare for the future

*"Look back at our struggle for freedom, trace our present day's
strength to its source; and you'll find that man's pathway to glory
is strewn with the bones of the horse."*
—Anonymous

*T*he Whale Whisperer is about many journeys undertaken within one greater journey: a journey that leads me back home. My greatest wish in sharing my journey with you is that it will help to reawaken your deeper knowing in reconnecting you with Mother Earth and its extraordinary diversity and beauty. We have to start honouring ourselves and the planet we live on, respecting her and all her children, for we are all connected, and the only thing that will save us is *love*. I have been so blessed on my journey, by the teachings of so many incredible creatures who have nurtured my trust and helped me shake off my self-doubt and overcome my fears. The more I have been taught, the more I realize that there is something much bigger. I'm constantly being told by the animals to look at the bigger picture and I'm guided to remind many clients, whom I perform readings for when their beloved pet has passed. I have had so much evidence that we all share our journeys with a soul group through different lifetimes. These include the animals that join us in our many incarnations and come back to us in different guises to continue their loving guidance. I was 'told' this by Sam, the Jack Russell puppy who was the catalyst in remembering my intuitive telepathic abilities. He was the first creature that 'talked' to me, which was strange enough, but he also talked about reincarnation, which was almost a step too far in the infancy of my re-awakening and almost made me doubt my sanity!

Before I recount my adventures around the world, I feel compelled to tell you about the wonderful journey the horses have shared with me, for they have been the catalysts and tutors of my re-acquired healing skills.

In my first book *An Exchange of Love*, I described how the horses taught me the shamanic practice of soul retrieval; how a traumatized fragment from the past could be reunited with the present animal or person, in order to make them whole once more. I believe they were re-connecting me with a shamanic past life, where I once had this knowledge. It was time to wake up, remember, so that I could embark on my journey of rediscovery in order to facilitate the re-awakening of others. The animals tell me that we are running out of time. The planet needs our help now. So many horses came into my life, teaching me the techniques that I needed to learn in order to be part of something much bigger – a small component, but part of the whole reawakening that is so vital at this time in planetary history. With the help of the animals, who are so much more in tune with the earth's resonance, we can all be part of something wonderful that we can co-create on our beautiful planet. I have had cases where horses had suffered terrible past-life battle trauma. I was introduced to Woody, the skewbald gelding, who 'showed' me a horrific video-like clip in my mind of his terror at the battle of the Somme in the First World War. Many others came to teach me about the need to heal man's warring obsession, and inhumanity to his fellow man. These horses were reincarnating to bring about change. I asked my guides why I was getting so many of these traumatic cases. My answer was that horses carry the war consciousness of man. We have ridden these loyal servants into battle throughout millennia and they have carried us and pulled our implements of death and have died beneath us. There are so many Equine Assisted Therapy centres springing up around the world, where the horses are the therapists, bringing gentle joy to disadvantaged children and adults.

Recently the horses have been teaching me a new technique. The old saying 'when the pupil is ready the teacher will appear' is so true for me, as the animals have 'tutored' me every step of my re-awakening. Animal's human companions are also being re-awakened and healed by them facilitating the memory of a shared past life trauma, not only remembering, but re-writing the outcome – a previous outcome that was colouring and limiting their present lives, either emotionally or physically or both! By changing the outcome, the need to hold the trauma within the cellular memory no longer existed, and so the physical or emotional symptoms had no place and could be finally released. Alberto Villoldo writes about this technique in his book '*Mending the past and healing the future with soul retrieval*', where he describes timelines and a rewriting of one's destiny. Horses know all about this because they've been a part of our trauma. I believe that the horses are showing this now so that we can journey into our futures and make the planet whole again. The more I have connected with the different species around the globe, the more I realize that each section of the collective consciousness of animals seems to have contracted into performing different tasks in order to bring about planetary healing. The following is a case study that was, up to now, one of the most dramatic I had experienced and illustrates beautifully how our pasts can limit our futures and cloud our present vision, both physically and emotionally.

"...and I whispered to the horse, trust no man in whose eye
you don't see yourself reflected as an equal."
—Don Vincenzo Giobbe

Seamus, Mary and Raj

Seamus was a dappled grey horse who nervously stomped and snorted as I reassured him that I was there to help. His owner had called me out to resolve his escalating fears about being loaded into horseboxes. Something told me that there was an issue worrying Seamus far more than walking up the ramp into his horsebox. I tuned in telepathically and he showed me a chestnut horse that he was really concerned about. The owner said that it could be her daughter Mary's horse Raj, who was becoming unpredictable to the point where she feared for Mary's safety. After performing some emotional healing on Seamus, I agreed to return to take a look at Raj.

When I entered the barn some weeks later I was greeted by Seamus, who nodded his head towards a large, powerful-looking chestnut at the end of the building. He said, as clear as day in my head, "For goodness sake, sort them out! They've got real issues". I thanked Seamus for his help and told him that I would do my best.

Raj eyed me suspiciously as I neared his box, with Mary next to him as she held his halter rope. She recounted some of the issues she had been having with him, including a real problem with turning to the left. I connected telepathically with Raj and asked for his version.

"Mary needs to have more confidence in herself," he responded. "I need her to be a stronger leader for me. When she believes in herself, I can believe in myself."

A strange marking on Raj's right shoulder caught my eye. According to Mary he had been born with the mark and his previous owners had assured her there was no injury underneath. I tuned in to the energy of Raj's shoulder, and asked him if this was the cause of his concerns. Immediately I was shown pieces of metal shrapnel embedded there in memory form, and from experience of removing energetic objects from past life wounds, I knew these would be remnants of a long-distant trauma.

Raj flashed me images from the past life in question as I visualized plucking these invisible pieces of metal from his shoulder, before filling the area with white light. He was a powerful grey warhorse, charging through a Napoleonic battlefield bearing his rider — Mary as a man — through the carnage. Cannons were firing all around them with deafening booms, their plumes of acrid smoke vying with the stench of fear and death. Mary raised her sabre as Raj courageously plunged into the thick of battle. Suddenly they were hit as a cannon exploded, hurling them onto their left side and crushing Mary beneath her steed. Sadly Raj's shrapnel wounds were fatal but Mary managed to survive, albeit with a withered arm and weakened left side. As I received these images, Mary complained of a stabbing pain in her left shoulder, and both she and her mother looked increasingly perplexed as the sensation intensified.

I worked to remove the negative memory in Mary's arm and asked if she could imagine the scene that Raj had shown me. To her amazement and her mother's astonishment, she was able to describe every detail of her uniform and how they both looked in that lifetime. I'm always thrilled when the rider can do this, as I know we're on track with what the horse has shown me. She shared that she had always been very weak in her left arm and side, and part of her difficulty in steering Raj to the left was down to this subtle handicap. Her arm began to tingle as though something was shifting, then Mary said the pain felt stuck at the elbow. I asked Raj, who was now holding Mary in his gaze and quietly supporting her through the process, to help me clear the blockage. He seemed to be willing her on to clear the trauma so they could both be free.

I asked Mary to visualize little taps on the end of her fingers, and pretended to turn them on to release the energy. As I held her hand between mine, I pictured dark, treacle-like energy flowing out. Mary imagined it turning into daisies that floated up towards the sky, taking the trauma with them. She visualized the pain in her shoulder and a block in her head also turning into daisies, which either drifted up on the breeze or she blew out of her mouth. Interestingly, one homeopathic remedy for deep tissue trauma is *Bellis Perennis*, which comes from the daisy plant.

Next we needed to re-script Mary and Raj's battlefield trauma. I asked Mary to imagine a positive outcome, where they dodge the cannon fire and gallop swiftly to safety. Mary described the fear she felt, then the relief of having escaped unscathed from the battle. Just as she finished her description, she turned white as a sheet and collapsed, complaining of an intense nausea. At the same moment Raj gave a huge sigh, collapsed onto his straw and proceeded to snort and groan with his eyes closed.

As I had never seen such a dramatic response from either pet or owner before, and a sense of alarm shot through me. What on earth would Mary's mother think? I quickly checked my fears and reminded myself this was simply the result of a massive energetic shift in their cell memories, and both horse and rider needed time to adjust.

After we continued to visualize the new tingly energy filling the whole of Mary's arms, the colour returned to her cheeks and she could stand again. Raj was still out for the count. So we walked Mary up to the house to make her a warm drink and allow Raj to recuperate from all his hard work in peace. As we reached the house, Mary suddenly exclaimed, "Its better! My whole left side feels different, stronger. I don't believe it!"

When we gave her a cup of tea inside the house she said that she could squeeze the mug with her left hand. Mary had never even been able to make a strong fist before, and here she was, flexing and clenching her hand over and over again to prove it wasn't just a fluke.

Thrilled though we all were, there was still concern for Raj. As we tiptoed back into the barn, I heard Seamus say in my head, "Thank goodness, about time!" And there was Raj, leaning over his stable door, looking cool as a cucumber. His eyes shone with a new softness, and he exuded a sense of peace and happiness. Reassured that he was fit and well, I left Mary with instructions to allow herself and Raj plenty of rest over the next few days to allow their new personas to settle in.

When I next heard from Mary, she and Raj were going from strength to strength, giving each other the confidence they both needed and bonding as a team. And now Seamus, who in his wisdom had no doubt exaggerated his behaviour in order to get me called in for his stable mate, was loading beautifully. It is cases like this that leave me in awe of the intelligence and courage of animals, and their compassion both for their fellow four-legged friends as well as their owners.

"Horses carry the war consciousness of man.
You have ridden us into your battles throughout millennia.
We return to educate and heal your tainted souls."
Stated by Woody, a skewbald gelding

I have had so many new cases where the horses have facilitated healing on such profound levels, helping us to shake off our perceived limitations inflicted by our past memories. I believe many are deliberately returning in their present form, so they can be with their human soul mates again, with the intent of clearing the energetic remains of a death or injury that are keeping them both stuck on a physical or emotional level. When I journeyed with the whales and was told how they were imbuing the water molecules of the ocean with their love, it makes sense that as humans, so much of our physical bodies are made up of water, that if we start changing the way we feel by our thought processes and mindsets, we can change our body's vibrations. The healing power of the mind using techniques such as Psycho-Neuro Immunology, which heals the body through visualization, has achieved wonderful results with cancer patients. Emotional Freedom Technique uses statements where a person declares that they deeply and completely love and accept themselves and choose to release the need to feel an emotional or physical pain.

Masaru Emoto says that water shows us how to look much deeper into ourselves as we are reflected within the water's message. All life is reliant on the purity of water. He discovered the effect of positive thought or words on the structures of the water molecules. Beautiful thoughts, words and messages of love create beautiful patterns in the frozen water, whereas the opposite is found when negative words and thoughts are transmitted. The molecules examined under the microscope are seen to be formless and dark. The whales also talk about the healing for the earth, 'The Blue Planet', in that their love and healing infused into the molecules of the life blood of the earth is also impacting on the health of the planet. Isn't it amazing that the animals already know all this? Their healing is so profound, we must start to trust their wisdom, and they have so much to teach us about love, trust and forgiveness. We need to forgive ourselves and others, not condoning, but releasing our disempowerment, ceasing to give away that power and re-claiming it. Horses in particular want us to be re-empowered. The traditional meaning of the horse 'medicine' in

Native American belief is '*power*'. This is their task, they are the experts, having witnessed our past misdeeds, and they are lovingly nudging us forwards into a new paradigm. Or perhaps reminding us of our past skills when we believed in Animism, where all creation was felt to have a soul or spirit. The ancient indigenous people worshiped and drew strength from animals, trees, plants and rocks. They knew the value of the earth and everything that exists within it. In our modern civilization we have become so detached from this wisdom and become disempowered because of it. Here and now the animals are working, through their messages of love, to bring us back on track. The wonderful film *Avatar*, viewed by thousands, shows how they connected to the 'horses' and dragon like creatures in telepathic communication and the importance of honouring their planet. I wonder if members of the audience, sitting there with their 3D glasses on, realized how expanded they have been by the concepts of the film, and what perfect timing for the message to be experienced by so many people.

My first adventure
and my lion connection

I'd only ever been on the usual tourist holidays, which were just a pleasant escape and respite from life's challenges. When I was married, with a herd of pedigree milking goats to look after, I didn't have a holiday for seven years. I also helped my veterinary surgeon husband run his busy practice, so there was no room for any time away from work. I felt I'd achieved very little in my life, except to have three fantastic children, and share my life with some wonderful animal companions. I had always been obsessed with animals, enjoying the bliss of snuggling into the neck of a horse, having a pet mouse run up my sleeve, and the unconditional adoration of a dog. Animals had always been a huge part of my life and I loved the interaction of my children with our animals, as they learnt about respect and caring for another sentient being. The animals gave them so much love and patience and in some cases extreme tolerance! I hadn't had much success with human relationships, but now realize that some of the gifts that I have been given, came from them.

Having had some breeding problems with one of the members of my Caprine herd, I attended an animal healing weekend, hoping that I might learn something to help my goats. There I learned to meditate for the first time and discovered that we are all healers, and something changed inside me. I had the best night's sleep that weekend that I'd had for ages, and felt that I was on the verge of something very important in my life. I started attending meditation classes, and a spiritual healing group.

After a couple of years, I met a new friend who had returned from America having learnt new past-life regression techniques. She asked if I might be interested in being regressed, to which I agreed. During the regression, I was taken back to an Egyptian lifetime, where I found myself as a priestess in a temple called Karnak. I had never heard of Karnak and was most surprised to find afterwards, that there was indeed a temple of that name.

In my regression, I was lured away from my healing work by the love of a man, who led me away from my temple work to live a nomadic life in the desert. I loved him dearly, but always felt remorse at deserting my healing abilities and duties. I had experienced a meditation some time before, where I had entered a temple through a walled entrance and then walked in between numerous huge columns. I found myself in a central courtyard and then turned left to enter a small inner sanctum. Inside was a large stone plinth. I lay on top of the cold stone and then transformed into someone else, wearing flowing garments. I had black braided hair and unusual jewellery. I suddenly felt the pull of a man's energy, almost drawing me through the temple walls. I ran outside and found him holding two horses; he was waiting for me to run away with him. We mounted the horses and galloped off over the sand duned horizon. Of course this felt wonderfully romantic and was not a meditation that I was in any hurry to come back from! I wasn't sure whether I was supposed to be having those kinds of thoughts and that I should be applying myself to more spiritual matters. I hadn't thought about this meditation for a couple of years, so it was very strange to find that I was able to feel so much emotion and have such clarity of my surroundings in the regression. The one overriding feeling when reflecting on that ancient lifetime was the feeling of guilt at shirking my duties, and when I 'asked' myself about my current incarnation, I was 'told' that this time around I had to do the work. I had to release my feelings of guilt and inadequacy, reclaim my abilities, and get on with it! I came away from the session rather unsure of how I should proceed. I had a husband and family and although I had dabbled a little with healing since my course, I didn't really believe that this was something I could do. Imagine my amazement, when a week later I received a spiritual book club magazine, and when casually glancing at the spiritual retreats and journeys page, one advert leapt out from the page at me. *'Egypt calls... Egypt calls once again to the Priests and Priestesses of*

Karnak. *The time has come to take your rightful place. Reclaim your ancient wisdom.'*
I shook from head to toe. I knew I had to find a way to go!

I immediately rang the number on the advert. My stomach was
performing summersaults and then a lady called Jehane answered. We
talked at length about our connections and feelings about Egypt and both
decided we knew each other. We were like dearest friends who hadn't seen
each other for a while, from about 3,000 years ago! The more we chatted
the more I knew I wanted to go to Luxor. The trip was planned for six
weeks time, so I had to find a way to finance it and talk to my husband to
see if he minded me going to Egypt for a week, leaving him with animals
and children. Surprisingly my husband was not horrified. He knew that I
had always wanted to visit Egypt without really knowing why.

My husband kindly drove me to Gatwick and we were met by Jehane
and the group of people who had been drawn to make the journey. Jehane
was very efficient with tickets and itineraries, but I think my husband was
bemused by other members of the group which he perceived as pretty
'flaky'. Perhaps alarm bells started to ring at that time for him. I'm not
sure, but he definitely didn't realize the profound effect the following
week was to have on me and how I was to return a very different
person from the wife and mother that he dropped off at the airport that
morning.

When we started to fly over the huge expanse of the Theban mountains
of the desert and I saw the famous Nile meandering beneath us, I could
feel the energy shift in me and I started to feel incredibly excited with a
sense of 'coming home'. Stepping out into the intense heat and bright
sun of Luxor and placing my feet on Egyptian soil was almost too much
for me to absorb. Was this just a whim? Was I being really selfish? What
was I going to find when I went to Karnak and how would I feel? Would
it be all that I hoped? And would it change my secure, safe, existence
back in England? This was so out of my comfort zone, travelling with
strangers, who seemed to understand their purpose far more than I.
I had to keep pinching myself to believe that I was actually there. I could

feel the Nile drawing me and I was desperate to experience sailing on her. The sailing feluccas and paddle steamers lined the docks and the palm trees had lights draped around their trunks, gently waved their welcome. We were serenaded off our bus by grinning musicians, forcing us to skip to the tantalizing, infectious rhythms, impossible to ignore, and we all involuntarily began to dance! I shall never forget entering the cool, dazzling interior with fountains and sparkling marble floors. I sat on the marble seat next to the fountain and started to believe I was really there.

We had a briefing about the next day's agenda, which was to be a visit to the temple at Luxor, starting at six o'clock in the morning to avoid the tourist rush. We were lucky enough to have Mohammed working with us, who was the chief inspector of antiquities and an Egyptologist. He was to facilitate our entry into areas normally prohibited to casual visitors and he gave us information about what we were going to see. We could hardly wait until the next morning, and I tossed and turned in my strange bed, trying not to disturb my room-mate. I was being deafened by a voice in my head that kept saying "Hator will help you, Hator will help you". I had no idea who or what Hator was, but as I was not going to be allowed to forget it after my disturbed night, I determined to question Mohammed as soon as we met in the morning.

As we alighted from the minibus and found ourselves walking down the ancient stone slab pathways, I was deafened once again in my head, by the 'ohm' sound, resonating continually in my brain. There seemed to be such a thin veil that we passed through into ancient times and every cell seemed to begin to revert back to a past incarnation imperceptibly with each step. The huge statues and obelisks towered over us and the ram's head sphinxes stared out into the distance with an enigmatic expression. We were told that they once lined the pathway leading to Karnak, connecting the temples. They had long since been overtaken by modern life as the town had expanded and many of them had been destroyed. I asked Mohammed who Hator was and he explained that the Egyptian pronunciation of Hathor was Hator. I had heard of this goddess but had very scant knowledge of anything, just a burning desire to remember and re-awaken my prior wisdom of these matters. I was grateful that I had been 'told' she would help me and wondered how that might unfold for me as the days passed. I only now realize the power of the energy and gifts I was given at her temples of Denderah and Deir El Medina. As we went deeper into the temple complex, we began to be affected by the power of the temple's energy. We chanted and toned in the grounds. It was wonderful being the only visitors so early in the morning when the temple felt pristine and bathed in ancient energy. Our quiet reverence seemed to preserve the ancient feel. I felt very hot, not due to the sun's rays but something much more powerful. I started to visualize my body being stripped of its flesh, as though I was standing in fire, and all my past traumas and lifetimes since this ancient time were being burnt away. My skeleton seemed bleached white as I was cleansed of all pain; we were all feeling a sense of transformation. I felt I was almost tumbling down an Alice in Wonderland tunnel, as different incarnations and personas of me flashed past. I was also re-united with the painful memory of a miscarriage in my current life. I was told that the child I had lost was an ancient soul, who had lived with me in my Egyptian life and that it had just wanted to experience being in my energy and part of me, and that it was not meant to incarnate fully at that time. I began to shake and sob as I had felt such grief at losing my baby, but I felt reassured and loved and that everything had a time and a place and that all was in divine and perfect order. I thought to myself that if nothing else happens on this trip, then it has been worth coming for in order to get closure and healing on this very painful experience. All of us had very profound, transmuting experiences, purifying the past pains that we had collected through millennia in our different incarnations.

After lunch we rested by the pool, digesting our meal and the early morning's revelations. We were due to meet later for a meditation and debrief of the morning visit to Luxor temple. Sipping fresh mango juice, we all felt such peace and a sense of connection to that ancient land. Swimming in the cool water as the temperature rose also seemed to add to our sense of purification. We finally dragged ourselves away and changed into more suitable clothes for our meeting. We were invited to call in the ancient deities, of whom I knew little about, nevertheless the room seemed to fill with other energies as they appeared to whisper and integrate into our own bodies. We were asked to visualize floating in the middle of a Merkabah, a sacred geometric shape, where two pyramid shapes join to form a six pointed star. I felt 'held' in the centre and we were asked to create an image of what we wanted for Egypt and how we might create a healing image for this wonderful country.

Firstly I was shown a golden ball with wings, which allowed it to fly through the air. It was flying through a starlit sky, with one very bright star shining out of the cosmos. Then the solid ball became a kind of filigree framework wrapped around the earth. It was tilted on an axis and it looked like the wings were trying to bring the planet back into balance and a more upright position. I later recognized the wings as similar to the wings that the goddess Isis holds outward in her many statues that we were to see in the stalls of the medina. On my return to England, I deciphered the vision and painted it, to anchor its message in reality. The rest of the day was spent in the markets, buying our white temple wear and trying not to spend all our money on the fabulous souvenirs that beckoned us at every corner.

We attended the sound and light show at Karnak that evening and I had to admit to being disappointed when we first arrived at the main entrance. We were very much part of a tourist show. It felt disrespectful as people swarmed over the ancient ruins. Although I had a fleeting vision of chariots and wild looking horses with flowing manes and flared nostrils, thundering through the temple gates, with all the colours and banners gleaming in the light, I just felt sad that this beautiful place had been brought to this. It felt sullied, desecrated and disrespected, as though few realized the true wonder of the ancient site. We all fell into our beds at the end of the evening, exhausted from the sheer roller coaster of emotions that the day had brought. Once again we left the hotel bright and early to revisit Karnak. This time my feelings were very different. I never expected to cry quite so much on that trip and at times it felt like my eyes had turned into taps that were constantly pouring water!

A dramatic return

Having arrived at the main entrance once more, I questioned the validity of my connection with this ancient city. The huge entrance with the avenue of sphinxes did not seem to really connect to any memories and I began to wonder if it I'd really got it all wrong and that perhaps this was all nonsense. That was until we entered the central courtyard and I looked to the left. There was the walled entrance with the pillars that I had seen in my meditation almost three years earlier and I knew without doubt exactly where I was going next! I kept straight on, some of the others wondering where I was going, so I said "I know where I am".

Entering a small inner sanctum, I came across the large stone plinth that I had laid on when I transformed into the priestess of Karnak, 3000 years before. I fell across the plinth wailing. Luckily there were no other visitors, as we all began to feel very emotional. Mohammed seemed a little surprised at the depth of our reactions and was even more amazed when many of us told him where sacred areas were and where more artefacts might be found, as each of us began to remember different aspects of our past lives there. As I sprawled across the plinth, I began to get a sense of the man I had fled my duties for, all those years ago. I could feel his energy drawing me through the walls, as he must have done when I strived to continue my healing work despite my love for him. I was struggling to contain myself as I sank down shaking and wondering if I could feel this level of emotion and love for this man, what if I met him in his re-incarnated form in this life? How would that affect my marriage, or perhaps it was showing me that I shouldn't be married now and that I

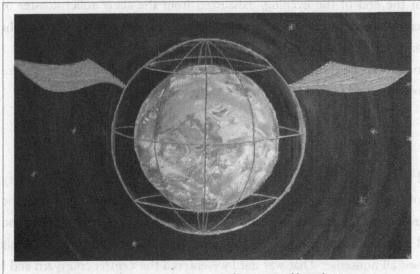

The vision which I painted on my return home — my goldengrid painting

should be concentrating on my healing work in this life? I felt as though he was almost sucking me through the walls as he waited with the horses, imploring me to join him. The rest of the group seemed concerned at the extent of my reaction. It was as though I ached to be with him and I knew I could no longer resist him in that past life. I had grabbed my opportunity and galloped away with him. I could visualize him so clearly with his flowing robes and dark flashing eyes. This time he could feel my resolve as I refused to join him. I sent a mental image of the message that I could not fail this time; I had to complete my healing duties. His sorrow drowned me in waves of emotion as I felt him beg me to join him once again. I had to deny my love for this mortal being and remain with the work of the deities that I had been an initiate with. Eventually through my tears, I was given an image of him turning and leading the horses away as he finally understood my message. I could almost taste the sand in my mouth, as I saw the wind blow his footprints and the hoof prints of the horses, away from the dunes that he climbed, away into the desert and I knew that he was gone for good.

The images were so intense – it felt so real, but how could it? I struggled to make sense of it all. It was so strange, stepping through the veil back into modern life with buffets and pool menus and the tourist spots of shops and bazaars. The smells of spices and the intense colours of clothing, scarves and rugs brought us back into another reality. All of us were feeling shell-shocked so we rested for the remainder of the day. It also became clear that the group had collective memories of being together at that time, especially on the next day's visit to Denderah.

Denderah

We were all excited at the prospect of being on the Nile as we stared at the wonderful scenery that passed by, little changed for hundreds of years, as people toiled in the fields trying to scratch an existence. Buffalo and donkeys were everywhere and children waved from the banks. The roofless homes revealed a very simple life with few possessions, shared with hens and a few goats. I reflected on how much I had at home and of the stresses of modern life and how our possessions seemed to own us in our materialistic world. Their life, although harsh at times, seemed so uncomplicated and their smiles made me feel as though they found happiness in being so connected to the earth.

Just being on that glorious river, conjured up such imagery from the past, I imagined all the river traffic that would have passed along this route throughout millennia. It was so beautiful but also I felt it was affecting me on such a deep level, and I felt certain that I had sailed down this river many times in previous incarnations. I was shown a kind of woven reed vessel with a very pointed bow. Some members of the group were also there with me and we were dressed in white, though a sense of sadness at separation was a common theme among us.

When we finally arrived at our destination, the beautiful temple of Hathor at Denderah, we disembarked in a flurry of anticipation. We entered the temple complex, and stood gazing in awe at the marvellous spectacle. Hathor greeted us, standing in her glory with her cow's ears and gentle smile. I could see why she was the goddess of dance, healing and joy: she looked so welcoming. As we entered the huge entrance with Mohammed explaining some of the history of the temple, we craned our necks and stared in wonder at the reliefs on the ceiling, still intense with wonderful hues and mysterious hieroglyphs, which spelt out ancient messages which we struggled to decipher. We were introduced to another Mohammed who was the chief guard and he arranged for us to sip hibiscus tea in a beautiful area with date palms. We climbed up the steps to the higher levels and lay beneath the incredible gold astrological chart. It was credited with being the first of its kind and we marvelled at the designs and the energy it was emitting. We had a strong sense of the goddess Isis joining us, and Jehane channelled her wisdom as we lay on the hard stone floor full of rapture at our experiences. As we descended the steps, we took time to explore. I found myself alone, studying the reliefs, when suddenly I was joined by the guard Mohammed. He beckoned me to follow him around the side of the temple to make our way to a special inner sanctum that was hidden from the usual tourist's view. I was uncertain, and aware that we were far away from anyone else, but then I felt that I should just trust and see what unfolded. We first stopped at a nilometer, a measuring device to gauge the level of the Nile. He dipped his hand in the water and seemed to want to anoint me with it. It felt very special and I felt honoured by his attention. He then asked if I would like to receive healing from Isis. I said I would be truly blessed if that was so. We scrambled over some fallen stones and came across a metal barred entrance to a small room with a rectangular opening in the roof, where the sun blazed through. He positioned me under the opening so that the light would shine down on my heart area. He said that he felt I needed healing in my heart. I didn't feel that I was too damaged emotionally at that time, but I felt that I was given strength and courage and my whole being seemed to expand. Little did I know how my life was to be totally turned upside

The beautiful temple of Hathor at Denderah

down and that I was to need all that strength and courage very soon. Finally I felt that I was ready to leave the loving healing rays of Isis and we locked the room and found our way back into the main complex. He showed me an opening into an underground catacomb area which was very confined and dark and I again allowed an element of fear to invade my thoughts. I was cross with myself as I knew it was yet another wonderful opportunity, but my fear of confined spaces overrode my decision to enter. So sadly I declined, but thanked him profusely for the honour he had bestowed on me.

A few minutes later we were joined by our own Mohammed and other group members. The guard opened the entrance once again to invite us down. Some of the group took one look at the tiny passage, and refused to enter. I was still feeling as though I really should have taken the opportunity to experience everything made available to me, so I agreed to go down. It was an extremely tight space, and I did doubt whether I had made the right choice, but once we were inside the larger space and saw how beautiful the reliefs were, my fears evaporated. The freshness of the designs and colours looked as though the paint was still drying and you could imagine the artists collecting their brushes and admiring their craftsmanship with satisfaction. It was also very hot and stuffy, so we scrambled back to the surface, keeping the pictures in our minds of the wonders in that incredible place. We felt somehow re-connected from our visit. Some members of the group had a collective memory of working at Denderah in far off times and we all felt that something very profound had affected us, by visiting this wonderful temple and that Isis and Hathor were directing us to re-discover our ancient pasts.

We celebrated our visit with a sumptuous Egyptian feast, prepared by Mohammed's mother. I have never tasted fish as good, before or since and we all felt full of energy as we laughed and chatted about our amazing experiences of the sacred place. The sight of the sun slipping into the horizon was magical and we imagined that we could just detect a slight hiss as the sun appeared to slip into the water. I lay in my bed smiling as I imagined still being on deck and feeling the motion of that iconic river, rising and falling, beneath me. Everyday had been more amazing than the last, but the next day where we were destined to return early in the morning, back to Karnak, proved to be the most life-changing.

There was a statue dedicated to the Egyptian god Khepri and it was prophesized that if you walked around the statue seven times, your wish would come true. So I thought I'd give it a try. I was asking to be shown the best way forward in my healing and that it be for the very highest good. On my second or third circuit of the statue, I was astounded to find my dog Pillow dominating my mind, and I could see her clearly wagging her tail and looking very happy. She had been the most beautiful blue merle collie cross who had been killed in the road outside our house. She was very young and we had all been devastated. This was emotional enough, but when she went on to tell me that she had died in order to address my issues with guilt, it was almost too much to bear. She told me I had carried this through many lifetimes since my Egyptian life, possibly 3000 years before, and now it was time to finally let go and resume my healing skills and fulfil my purpose. The rest of the group that I had met were shocked at my floods of tears as I tried to tell them what had occurred. My whole week in Egypt was very emotional as I remembered so much of my previous lives there.

A year later, I returned to Karnak with two other members of the group that also shared lifetimes with me and we had decided to return to further deepen our connections with that ancient land. Once again I decided to walk around the statue, this time just asking to be shown the best way forward after a very difficult time since my mother's death.

As before, I had no thought of Pillow, I was concentrating on the recent traumas in my life. But there she was again large as life in my mind, wagging her tail and laughing at me. She said I was doing really well with releasing my guilt and that she was very happy in spirit and glad that I was doing the work that I was meant to be after all this time. Again I was in floods of tears with her love that she shared with me, but this time I tried to share her joy. I was so glad to see she was happy and free in spirit. I determined that I would persevere with my healing work and not fail this time in my commitment to be of service to others. I was able to reflect on how I had been kept on track thus far, thanks to the animals.

Sekhmet

It makes me smile now as I recall my experiences in that short week of my life. I was so innocent and ignorant on the surface, stumbling through the mists of time, trying to remember who I really was. I felt I had led such a insignificant life, muddling through disastrous relationships, bogged down with mundane issues. I wonder if I'd really known the effect my next encounter would have had on me, whether I would have entered into it so readily and unsuspecting? I know that I had to find my destiny, and take up the reins of my life, finally accepting my life's purpose.

It was another early start as we climbed aboard the horse drawn kaliesh. Mohammed had felt that it might be a treat for us to sample a different form of transport. The beautiful, but painfully thin Arab horse stomped as we seated ourselves. It bore the marks of old harness sores on its back and we pleaded with the driver not to whip its lacklustre sides. The horse drew us dutifully through the streets of Luxor. We asked the driver what the horse was called, and he said her name was Princess. We said that we would pay him extra if he would feed her more food to reward her for her toil, because if she looked well-kept and cared for, more tourists would be drawn to use his carriage. We somehow hoped this might persuade him to take better care of her and that at least one horse might benefit from our good intentions. I felt quite ashamed to be sitting in the carriage, as though I was condoning the treatment of the horses. I had spent all my life loving horses and hated to see them so abused. We were thrilled to find them on our return visit, a year later, resting in a side road, and immediately recognized the driver and Princess's slightly crooked white 'star' on her forehead. Princess was really living up to her name. Her chestnut coat gleamed and her harness shone, as her driver proudly waved at us. We congratulated him on how wonderful she looked, and what a great job he'd done. He obviously recognized the slightly demented English women who'd given him a bit of a lecture the year before!

Anyway, Princess drew us to the temple entrance where we dismounted and underwent the usual security checks. We were all dressed in our white garments with shawls to cover our heads.

Walking through the empty temple, we turned to exit through 'my entrance' and found a path that meandered through the grounds and led to an area quite separate from the main complex. On entering the dark rooms, our eyes adjusted to the change and we encircled the statue of Ptah. We chanted and toned and felt such a rush of energy through our bodies. I had no previous knowledge as to who Ptah was, but the effect of connecting with him could not be ignored as we began to shake and once again felt our bodies being re-arranged. However stepping through into the next inner room, we were greeted by a tall, black lion-headed statue. I was instructed that this was Sekhmet who was claimed to be the wife of Ptah, and she was the warrior goddess that created order through chaos. We took it in turns to place small flowers as an offering to her and when it was my turn, I felt drawn to just place my hand lightly on her heart centre. I was not prepared for the effect that had on me. It was as though I rushed back through time and was shown leonine beings, which seemed half-lion, half-human. I felt Sekhmet communicating through me and she told me that I was her daughter and a keeper of the ancient lion being wisdom. I felt her place her hand on my heart and she said "I am in your heart now and you will take me home with you. You are Arashneemadaan, High Priestess of the lion beings from Sirius". I started to cry as my emotions overwhelmed me. It was a strange mix of disbelief perhaps of the ramblings of a vivid imagination, and the certainly of how real it all felt. I shuddered as I felt her presence in the centre of my heart, like a small weight. I recalled a past life regression group where I had visualized myself as a young Massai boy seeking to enter manhood by killing a lion. I had failed miserably and was banished from the tribe. The group facilitator had said that perhaps I wasn't meant to kill lions and that perhaps some part of me prohibited that act. I began to think that perhaps she had been right after all? Perhaps my Egyptian and, even stranger, other planetary origins, would prevent me from causing any harm to a lion! As we stepped out into the sunshine, a part of me wondered whether I had just imagined it all. It seemed so fantastical that I would have been this being that carried the wisdom of this ancient race. Who did I think I was to think such things? Yet I could still feel the weight in my heart. I almost forgot my ancient name, in my disbelief. However that night instead of Hathor shouting in my ears, I had Sekhmet almost shrieking at me and repeating my name over and over so I wouldn't forget or dismiss it. I felt her frustration as I struggled with the whole concept. So I felt I had to find out more about her and the lion beings, on my return, and try to fulfil my duties, whatever they might be this time around.

The rest of the trip was filled with visits to the bazaars to buy gifts and we had a fantastic balloon ride over the Valley of the Kings. I was normally afraid of heights, but seeing the temple at Luxor bathed in the rosy glow of the sunrise dispersed all anxiety. I marvelled at the swathe of fertile land running parallel to the Nile, nurtured by its flood and then, only yards away, arid dessert desiccated by the full force of the Egyptian sun.

Our triumphant landing on the edge of a sugar cane field was applauded by the ground crew as they drummed and sang in celebration. We were then collected by the minibus and taken to the tombs, where we melted as we visited King Tut's resting place in the midday heat. We climbed down deep into the tomb, staring with wonder at the reliefs and thinking what it would have been like to discover this, and the tales of the curse as they breathed the fetid air from a long sealed grave. It was a wonderful sight and we felt some magical beings join us as we sang our tones which echoed through the tomb. We felt that the builders and craftsmen had stepped out of the walls to join us in admiring their work! We also saw the huge temple of Hatshepsut on route, but we wanted to visit another smaller Hathor temple at Deir el Medina. Again the image of Hathor smiled out at us, beckoning us in, as we were greeted by the temple guard. He allowed us to explore the inner sanctums in peace and seemed to know that we were there to respect the temple and a few words from Mohammed confirmed this for him. As we stood inside the holy of holies, I had some very strange sensations. One of our group began to channel ancient Egyptian, which sounded very familiar and then it was as though my head had been opened up and keys of wisdom were being dropped inside, descending into me like a bottomless well. I had no idea what they were or what they meant, but I knew it must be very important. I felt sure that in the future I would come to know what they symbolized.

On our return visit a year later, I was to be given even more profound gifts from this magical place, but for now our week was nearly over. We had more debriefs and meditations and our last evening was spent eating a delicious meal and watching another glorious sunset. I would miss the beautiful blue sky and the warmth of the sun on my skin. Everything else seemed almost too much to comprehend and needed a lot of assimilating. The thought of being home back in Britain seemed so alien, I knew it would take some re-adjustment.

As we landed at Gatwick, the energy in England felt so heavy as though we were moving through treacle. It was difficult to disconnect from the group, having shared many emotional reconnections from our past lives together. Egypt had become my reality and England felt foreign and unfamiliar. We tore ourselves away from each other, and then I spotted my husband waiting patiently for me, looking disconcerted at the levels of emotion the group members were showing each other. Promising to keep in touch, we parted company and my husband and I started the journey home. I wondered how much I should try to explain about my experiences, but he seemed angry at the change of completion dates for our house move which was scheduled for the following week. I had hoped to recoup a little energy over the weekend, but now it seemed that we would be in a frenzy of packing and cleaning. He didn't seem very interested in my experiences and even trying to explain any of it seemed pointless. I had experienced a strange dream a few months before my trip, where I got the distinct impression that we were not going to make it as a couple, but I dismissed it as just a silly dream and that of course we were fine. Everything seemed perfect on the surface. We had a lovely house in the country, and after some challenges with the children they now seemed to be happy and doing well. We were set for life – weren't we?

The house move was very stressful and I longed to be back in Egypt and close to that ancient energy that had reclaimed my being. It didn't help that the house we moved into was filthy, so we had days of cleaning and scraping grime and my husband seemed to get grumpier. At regular intervals I would get calls from the group members, all of us struggling to make sense of our respective journeys and how they were impacting on our mundane lives back in England.

My mother had not been well for some time and had had one operation to remove a tumour, which we hoped would cure her cancer. However, her health had deteriorated and so I demanded that we see the specialist. She lived on her own and was not getting much help from the NHS, so she had more tests and scans and just before Christmas we went to get the results together. We sat in stunned silence when they announced the dreadful prognosis. We were told that the cancer had spread and that there was nothing they could do to help her. Chemotherapy was suggested, but they felt that she was already so weak that it would do nothing to improve her remaining few months of life. So I organized for lots of healing and took advice from cancer nutritionists and herbalists and did what I could to support her.

My fiftieth birthday was looming and I had previously booked a trip to swim with wild dolphins in Costa Rica for my birthday treat, as it had been a lifelong dream of mine. We'd had a weekend in Venice as a romantic break just for the two of us. It had been so stressful for me over Christmas

A relief of the Egyptian goddess Hathor

as my dear mum didn't want me to tell anyone about her illness and have their Christmas spoiled, so I had to keep it to myself and pretend that everything was fine and that she would be making a full recovery. The pressure of creating a happy Christmas for everyone, knowing that it would probably be her last, was excruciating. I adored my mother and I couldn't bear the thought of her not being there. I felt that she and my husband were my best friends. My husband had seemed very supportive at first, but the more time I spent trying to look after my mother, the more distant we seemed to become, so knowing that my mother was well looked after, I paid for us to have this break, but it did little to rekindle our relationship. I worried so much about my dolphin trip and didn't want to waste any precious moments with my mother, but she insisted that I went. However my stress levels created a very painful bout of shingles and so I was prevented from travelling. I was so grateful for that special time that we had together, but devastated at the level of pain my mother was trying to cope with. I lay in bed one night and pleaded for help. I felt that it wasn't my role to heal her, but that I was to help her pass with as little fear and pain as possible. She showed such courage and grace, but the pain was becoming unbearable. The problem was that the tumour was pressing down on and restricting the bowel. I was shown this in my mind symbolically, as a collapsed mine shaft. I was 'told' that I could place crystal pillars that would support the mine roof – like celestial 'pit props'. These crystals were like clear quartz, but with an inner fire. I called them light crystals. I visualized placing them in the mine shaft and saw the light illuminating the passage downwards. The next morning I rang my mother and was thrilled to hear that her pain had been much relieved during the night, and from then on, she felt no further pain in that area.

A few days later, my husband suddenly announced that he longer wanted to continue with our marriage but would give no reason for his decision. I was devastated as I had no idea that he felt so desperate about the decline of our relationship. We had never rowed and he had not verbalized any real discontent with my spiritual awakening. I asked him if he wanted me to give it all up, which I was prepared to do, in order to save our marriage, but he said that he felt driven to make that decision and nothing I could say or do would change his mind. I found it so hard to understand as he would give no reason and of course his timing could not have been worse. I knew my mother had just weeks left as her illness ravaged her body. I felt very angry and betrayed and so sad that it had come to this with a young son still relying on us both to be there for him. However I now realized that the universe was providing me with space to realize my healing duties. Losing both of them at the same time was incredibly hard to bear, and I wondered many times about the healing I had received at Denderah and perhaps that was preparing me for what was to come.

My beautiful mother passed on a lovely sunny day in July and with my husband gone, I didn't know how I was going to go on. The doctor commented on the lack of pain my mother had experienced towards the end, and I privately prayed that the light crystals had played a part in helping. I was grief-stricken. But my children and animals made me get up in the morning and to somehow function on the daily school runs and everyday chores that had to be done. I was also working with human and animal clients by then, and so threw myself into my work.

I was working with a gentleman one day who was not prone to channelling strange beings. He was a very grounded ex-naval officer, so I was astonished when we were working with a stress management visualization, he suddenly said, there's a strange person in my mind who has a message for you! Rather taken aback I asked what that message was. He said that this 'person' was from Atlantis and that the 'light crystals' worked and I had to believe in my skills as a healer. These crystals were used in my Atlantean past lives and that I had to remember this and to start using them more frequently. Of course he had no knowledge of the symbolic healing that I had sent my mother, so I was stunned with his revelations. We chatted about the message and it seemed that the Atlantean being also helped him to expand his awareness. He seemed very changed by his new-found channelling abilities and the healing he received from the ancient beings. I was shown new ways of working with light crystals over the coming months, as different cases came my way that would stretch my abilities and belief in the efficacy of these wonderful tools. I realize that I was so guided and protected through this time and many new beings started to enter my awareness. I connected with another Atlantean being who used a strange 'clicking' language and I felt a very specific energy when he came close, like a kind of tingling, that would run through my body in icy waves.

I had kept in close contact with two other people from our group and in the following autumn we decided to return to Egypt. I wanted to try and make sense of everything and to get clarity on the purpose of these very challenging life changes, as I was forced to cope on my own. Our youngest son found the fallout from the divorce and his grandmother's death very hard to cope with. My two other children also struggled, but were older and had their own lives to live. My son missed his father, so was happy to have extra time with him, as I left for another week. I knew he would be well looked after and I had to get some kind of reassurance that there was a purpose to all of this and that I hadn't just messed everything up on some stupid whim. I thought that going back to Egypt would help me understand the reason for all the chaos that had occurred in such a short space of time. We were also having to temporarily downsize and buy somewhere without a mortgage.

I was still feeling very fragile as we landed back in Luxor. It was wonderful to feel the energy shifts again as we flew in. The Nile sparkled beneath us and my spirits started to lift a little. We revisited Karnak and I had an emotional reunion with Sekhmet. I asked her why she seemed to have caused so much chaos in my life in one short year and couldn't she have spread my traumas out a little, rather than to be stripped of so much in so little time. She said there was no time to waste spreading my challenges out and that I had to get back on track and start working, using my ancient skills. She explained that the new vibrational shifts on the planet were making it imperative for us to clear our 'baggage' and anything that was limiting us from being our true authentic selves. It still seemed like a very high price to pay, but she reminded me that everyone else was on their journeys and that my husband needed to be free to find his own way. My mother had pre-agreed with me at a soul level to be a catalyst to bring about this change in my being, and that she had her own healing journey to travel. Again I seemed to spend most of my time crying!

I returned to Denderah and met Mohammed again. I was amazed that he recognized me and called me his daughter. I told him what had transpired in the year since we last met and I questioned him as to whether he felt the urgency of the healing strength of Isis, in order to prepare me for the roller coaster of events that were coming my way. He said that he had felt great sorrow and emotional pain around me, and was guided to take me to Isis so that she could prepare me. I also reflected on the chaos that had ripped my world apart after I had connected with Sekhmet. I prayed that some kind of 'order' would now unfold.

On our final visit to Karnak and to make our farewells to Sekhmet, I stopped once more by the scarab statue of the god Kephri. I had been told, the year before, that if you walked around the statue seven times and made a wish, it would come true. On the first occasion, my lovely dog Pillow had come through from spirit and reassured me that she was fine, but had passed in quite traumatic circumstances, in order for me to release all my issues of guilt that I had been carrying from so many lifetimes, but especially from the Egyptian lives. She had somehow managed to get out from our well fenced garden and had been killed by a motorbike. I had felt such guilt as I knew I should have checked the fencing more and maybe there had been some small opening that I had missed. There were also other reasons to feel guilty, as I had ignored another premonition about her. But here she was again, this time, bounding into my thoughts. She said she loved being pure energy. I asked her if she might return to me in a physical form. I had been communicating with animals and they had taught me about the concept of them returning to continue being with their human carers, in order to further guide and heal them on their combined soul journeys. She said that she didn't feel she would, but that she would continue to guide me from spirit and that I was doing very well and I had to keep going on my healing journey, both for myself and others. She said that she would be there to guide me whenever I doubted myself and that everything was as it should be. This was still very emotional for me to accept as it seemed that so little of the past *me*, remained.

We entered the small shrine to Sekhmet on our last morning and I felt drawn to wrap my body around her statue. I started to feel the Atlantean energy tingle through my body, and I started to 'talk' in a series of clicks, as I sank into a kind of trance, not really aware of the strange sounds emanating from my lips. My friend said that it felt like there were three beings holding a conversation through me, like some bizarre Morse code. I was later to be reminded of the sound when listening to the recordings of a sperm whale on my next adventure to the Azores, where the sound was almost identical.

We also revisited Deir el Medina where the 'keys' had been dropped into my being. This time one of the walls in the inner sanctum seemed to shimmer and become almost fluid in a strange greenish light. The hieroglyphs seemed to liquefy, as I visualized reaching my arm into the wall and finding that I was passing through seven layers, whereupon I grasped a very strange looking key. It had a long golden shaft, with intricate locking design protrusions and strange codes inscribed on it. I was guided to visualize placing the key into my heart, into which it seemed to slide effortlessly. We also felt joined by outer planetary beings that elevated us up through the temple roof as we were given healing and also received yet more healing techniques from our past long forgotten knowledge. One of my friends photographed the wall and to our amazement the hieroglyphs looked all blurred and the strange green light seemed to pervade the picture. However when the photo was printed, the wall seemed solid and 'normal'. It was a very powerful experience and

Mohammed, who anointed me with water from the Nile and performed healing on me at the temple of Hathor

I marvelled yet again at the profound affect this unassuming temple had had on us. Yet more evidence of the impact of Hathor on my life.

Our last visit was to another sacred place we had felt drawn to in Karnak. Past tall columns and statues, we entered another holy of holies. I felt a huge lion presence there. We seemed to be surrounded by lion beings. My two companions were also being deeply affected by their presence. Luckily no one else came into the room as the tourists were, by now, starting to fill the temple grounds. The universe again contrived to give us private time which, yet again, proved to be fortuitous as the lions who encouraged me to 'roar'! I felt the enormity of the sound building in my stomach. One of my friends was standing in front of me and the sheer volume of what came out of my mouth shocked me, and made my friend topple over. We were forced to lie on the floor as the roars continued to pour from my mouth. Any unsuspecting tourist would have immediately called for my mental health to be questioned! However we were alone except for many lions joining us as I felt them surround us. I felt like I was being instrumental in joining up my friends with their lion companion guides, which has happened on many occasions since then. My guides were a huge male lion, who stood on my right, and a fierce lioness on my left. I felt they were balancing and protecting the corresponding male and female sides of my body. They have worked with me ever since and helped with some very dark energies that I came into contact with. I have been asked to remove negative entities from people, animals and environments and whenever my lions have felt that it might affect my well being, they have stepped in and transmuted the energy from negative to positive. The male lion said his name was Shasti, pronounced Shaaarksti, and the female was called Latuna, pronounced Latoona. They were very precise and told me that I was just reconnecting with all my lion being skills and wisdom. This was still very early days in my re-awakening so it still seemed puzzling to me that I might be this being, inside my quite inconsequential human form.

Returning home this time still took some adjusting to and I knew I would still have to cope with everyday life and making sure my children were coping with the upheavals that a divorce brings to a family and also the continuing feelings of grief, as I missed my mother every day. I continued to be asked to work with an array of different clients that challenged and expanded my healing resources and I connected with new people who were on a similar spiritual wavelength.

Arizona, sun discs and the white buffalo

One of the new people I met was a lady called Magi. She worked with crystal skulls, one of which was an enormous citrine skull that she used in workshops and healing sessions. I finally painted the visions that I had received in Egypt, of several lion beings and the Earth in a golden grid. One of the lion being paintings contained an image of a leonine face with a heart shape over its mouth and the key that I had been given at Deir El Medina, in the heart's centre. A wonderful friend had given me a healing session where I had felt that I had returned to Sirius. All I felt was complete and utter love and everything was manifested by pure thought patterns. I saw how we, as beings, were sort of 'hatched' out of celestial white 'eggs' or pods. They seemed to just burst open and new perfect beings would alight from their gestation. I had a massive tantrum as I wanted to refuse to go back to the earth as I felt so battered emotionally. I felt that my human existence was too harsh and I wanted to remain in the pure love energy of my 'home'! I was told emphatically that I had more work to do and much to re-learn and that I had to go back. They removed my physical human heart and replaced it with a crystal heart that felt like it had a silver hue to it. It felt as though my human heart was worn out and that I needed a stronger replacement! I finally agreed to return with an emotional 'tens' machine that they agreed I could use if the going got tough! My new crystal heart was the one I painted, containing my Egyptian key. I felt that the lion being was me, and that I had to place a real quartz crystal on the shaft of the key that I painted in my heart. I tried to do this with the greatest respect to the crystal that I chose, as I always worried about 'gluing' crystals.

I felt drawn to show her the paintings and in a workshop that I attended with Magi, I visualized zooming into various places around the planet, as

I skimmed in and out of the golden grid that wrapped itself around the earth. She was very interested in the grid lines around the planet and also my lion beings. She said that she was embarking on a journey around America, using the crystal skull energy and creating a five pointed star of healing around Arizona and would I join her for that part of the trip. I had my travel fund from my dear mother, but I wanted to make sure that my son was alright. We had talked about going to Canada to ride on the Rocky Mountain railway, as he loved anything to do with trains, so I booked our trip later in the summer for us, and managed to escape for the week in January to meet Magi in Phoenix. I was very nervous about travelling on my own. I had never booked flight tickets by myself and wasn't sure why I was asked to go and what I could contribute. My worst fear was that I would land at the airport and she might not be there. I had no details of where we would be staying, as she said we would be guests of some new friends of hers who had kindly agreed to put us up.

It's amazing that the more you think about a fear, the more likely it is that you will manifest that fear in your reality. This was a prime example and was such a big lesson for me. I fretted all week before I travelled and during the flight about 'what if' etc... Here I was winging my way to an unknown destination *somewhere* in the area of Phoenix. I had never been to America before and it hadn't really been on my list of places to explore, but Magi seemed sure that I would play my part in helping somehow with the planetary healing work she had been guided to perform.

After we landed, I waited to collect my luggage but it never showed itself. I was the last passenger standing forlornly next to the carousel and I thought – what now? I found an airport employee and asked for help and they directed me to a desk, but I had to give the address where I was staying, so that once located they could return my errant luggage. Magi was nowhere to be seen either, so I couldn't ask her for the address of where we were spending the night. My mobile phone didn't work, so I was beginning to panic! Here I was in a strange country, with no luggage, no place to spend the night, and no one there to meet me. I contemplated jumping on the next flight back to England and hopefully track down my bags. Suddenly, in the midst of my despair, I heard a tannoy message blaring out my name, asking me to go to a public phone in the arrivals lounge. To my great relief it was Magi on the line, telling me that she was on her way! I was so relieved. Magi arrived and we were able to give an address for the airport to deliver my case to. I was by now feeling quite exhausted with all the emotional escapades of the past few hours. The airport personnel assured me that they would deliver it as soon as it arrived, but we didn't know where we were staying for the second night, so it was imperative that I had my suitcase that night. True to their word, they arrived with my wayward case later that evening.

We spent the night with a lady who was so kind in accommodating us. We breakfasted and awaited the arrival of yet another friend who was to drive us to Sedona. I had heard of the amazing energy vortexes there and was full of excitement at visiting this magical place. A knock at the door signalled her arrival and we loaded the car, thanked our kind hostess, and set off on our journey through the wonderful landscapes of cacti and red rocky outcrops.

It's an extraordinary place, wild and beautiful, the enormous cacti standing guard over the ancient Hopi Indian tribal ground. I had hoped to meet some First Nation people, but we had to complete our mission and intuit the correct places for us to place healing energy. I was guided to use the light crystal energy that I had first discovered when trying to help my mother. Since the first clear quartz-like crystal pillars that I had visualized, I had been 'given' many different types and colours of crystals. Sometimes they appeared like orbs. I had travelled to Silbury Hill in the UK, and felt drawn to place an etheric carnelian-like, red crystal orb onto the surface on the top of the hill. I had felt there was inner pyramid energy inside the hill, and that when the orb dropped down into that space it seemed to zigzag outwards throughout the whole area. There were also some very beautiful crop circles in the area and I felt that this was all connected somehow. There also seemed a connection with all the pyramid formations around the world, like a whole network of pyramid energy. I had been given crystal discs to place within animals and people, especially horses, which seemed to help any back complaints that they had, as I was guided to place them between vertebrae. I was also given a kind of light crystal massage gel, which I could visualize rubbing into a damaged area and again, which seemed to have very beneficial results. I might have looked slightly crazy, pretending to dip my fingers into an imaginary pot and then appear to massage an area about two inches away from the body. However, I learnt to trust my guidance and remember that 'light crystals work'! The first time I used this technique on a horse called Les it had almost instant pain relieving results. I have also been guided to pack an energy wound, where I may have removed a past life injury, like a spear, sword, or arrow. People and animals did seem to feel something being extracted and then soothed by a kind of soft light crystal wax plug.

When we arrived at a remote valley, we alighted from the car and walked around the rocky paths. We felt a very powerful vortex of energy and, stepping through, I felt I had grown several feet in stature and my whole body felt very different. I was guided to place some light blue orbs that seemed to be placed in my hands and I visualized them slipping through the surface of the ground and then their energy spreading outwards, again in a zigzag fashion. I was then 'shown' some enormous etheric golden discs, rather like the sun discs I had seen in Egypt, adorning Sekhmet and Hathor's head. These were rather like satellite dishes. I was guided to visualize placing six of the huge discs in an arc formation and then a final disc that would lie horizontally in the centre of the arc. This felt like it was giving and receiving information and that somehow the arc was channelling that information. I had no idea where these discs came from or who or what would be working with the information. I just performed my duties and prayed that this would be for the highest good of all concerned. The effect of the discs' energy seemed to illuminate the whole valley with golden light. I have since used much smaller versions of the sun discs to separate negative energy flow between people and animals, to facilitate a separation of energetic ties that might be impacting in a negative way, thus allowing both parties a chance to reclaim their energy and be re-empowered, rather than drained by the energy leaks.

We were lucky enough to be invited to stay with a Chinese woman who kindly allowed us to sleep in her mobile home. As it was January, the desert temperatures dropped dramatically at night and I awoke shivering in the early morning. I started to feel a very strange energy in the room. In the left hand corner, silvery teardrop formations seemed to be suspended in mid air. I rubbed my eyes, trying to determine what on earth I was imagining now. I suddenly had my mind filled with all kinds of strange words and images and I felt a presence enter my body. It was very gentle and I didn't really feel invaded, just very loved. I was told that this was Plaedian energy and that they had directed my sun disc implants and that they were thanking me for assisting them! I thanked them for helping me and offered to be of help whenever they might have need of me. I felt they were very healing and totally committed to helping us struggling humans and the planet earth. They told me that what happened on earth also impacted on all the planets and star systems. Again this all felt very real and important. When Magi woke up I excitedly told her about our 'guests'. She, of course, was well versed in all things outer planetary, but it was all very new to me. They then seemed to fade away, leaving us wondering what the new day would bring, and whether the Plaedians would join us again and give us more information.

After breakfast, we were joined by a mutual friend called Nick who was to drive us to the various areas we needed to visit. I was so excited as we were to visit the Grand Canyon, but first there was one more area we had to visit in Sedona. I had brought a small bag of quartz crystal points and although I was working with etheric crystals, I was drawn to bring them along on the journey. I placed a few crystals in the area of another valley and vortex and then Nick and I climbed a track to see some ancient cave paintings. We had noticed a flat surface in the high cliffs around the valley and joked that it looked like a kind of landing pad for spacecraft. As we were about to descend the steep track that had led to the caves, a man appeared out of nowhere. He pointed to the cliff top and said, "You see that flat mountain top; some people say it's a landing strip for Plaedian space ships"! Nick and I looked at each other and when we turned to look at the man again, he was gone. We looked up and down the track and there was nowhere he could hide, he had simply disappeared. We felt that perhaps he had just come as a messenger to reinforce the message that the Plaedians were very much in evidence in the area, and that they definitely had their finger on the pulse of the planet!

We travelled through the changing landscape, stopping to enjoy the spectacular view and the sheer magnitude of the canyon. None of us could find words that described our feelings. We knew we had to find another place on the rim to carry out our healing work, so we drove on and stopped next to a small tree that clung to the edge. In the distance, out in the canyon, was a huge pinnacle and it seemed to be a beacon of energy. We found out later that it was called the Isis point! This made perfect sense as the energy that started to fill us seemed very leonine and Egyptian. I placed the small bag of crystals on the earth by the tree, as I felt that they would absorb some of the energy that seemed to be eminating from the rocky point that dominated our vision. We started to chant and I began to feel more and more lion energy filling my being. I felt that I had to kneel on the ground on all fours, placing my hands in the soft soil, right on the rim of the canyon. I'm usually quite afraid of heights and the depths to which you could plummet if you slipped didn't bear thinking about! I started to feel that my shoulders had the fluidity of a hunting lioness and I could feel my whole body shape-shift into a lion. I felt so powerful, but then just as suddenly the feeling faded and I felt my human body revert. One of my hands had been placed on a rocky surface but the other had been placed in the dusty soil, almost on the edge of the rim. When I looked down to where my hand had been, I was shocked

The landscape of Sedona, a magical place

to see, not a hand print, but a large paw print. We all examined the print in amazement. I was still quite stunned by the experience, and thought perhaps it had been a group hallucination, but it had felt very real.

We journeyed on to the town of Flagstaff. Nick mentioned that he'd heard that there had been a white buffalo at Flagstaff, but he thought it had died. I lamented the loss of such a sacred creature and said that I would have loved to have seen it. He suddenly screeched to a halt and we all gasped in amazement as we saw a building with a sign emblazoned, 'Flagstaff, home of the white buffalo'. We thought perhaps it was a museum where they had pictures of the famous creature. We decided we would like to see them and learn more about what had happened, and whether there were any others that had been born, as we knew how important the return of the sacred beasts were to the First Nation people.

We went inside what seemed like a shop selling Navaho artefacts. The shopkeeper started to show us photographs of white buffalo and talked about various breeding programmes with ordinary brown buffalo that had the white gene and could then produce a white calf. I was somewhat puzzled as she seemed to be talking about several white buffalo that had been successfully bred. I still thought that this must be somewhere else and that this was just an information centre. I was thrilled to think that there were other white buffalo in existence. She then said "When you go outside, the first white buffalo you will see is...". I interrupted her and said "You mean they are here? Real live white buffalo?!" She gave me a look as if to say – what do you think I've just been talking about! I shall never forget stepping through the doorway into the fresh Arizona wind and the sight that met my eyes made me burst into tears. Right in front of me was a huge white buffalo mother and calf. There were several large brown buffalo and a couple of other white youngsters in the distance. All around the enclosure, the fence was adorned with flags and native fetishes celebrating the white buffalo presence. I was also interested to see some rather Egyptian looking motifs that looked distinctly leonine!

I had attended a drumming circle, where I had a vision of seeing a white buffalo being killed by white men. I had been a native who was supposed to be protector of the herd and I was heartbroken when I saw the buffalo fall from his wounds, and the life light fade from his eyes. I remember sobbing when I returned from the meditation, and I wondered if this was yet another past life that I had experienced. I felt that the fortunes of the tribe that had deteriorated after the loss of the white buffalo, mirroring the decline of the nations, as the vast herds were desecrated by the white man. I felt that at last they had returned and that perhaps the first nations could unite and be healed after years of separation from their territories and beliefs. The owner of the centre obviously still thought I was crazy and I apologized for my outburst, but I was so thrilled to see these magical beasts. I went to explore the enclosures and tried to tune into the mother of the calf, sending her all my love and gratitude for allowing me to meet her that day. She allowed me to touch her, her warm breath billowing across my palm, and then her calf came forwards. He nuzzled my hand and then I began to feel him direct words into my head, which I scribbled down so as not to forget them. I realized he was talking about the return of the white buffalo to heal mother earth, and he said:

"We are anchoring the life blood into the stones of our mother.
She wept at our loss. We come to remind you of what was lost. We come
to remind you of what was, and how you should honour our mother and
yourself. This is our message... learn it well."

I was blown away by the privilege of 'talking' with this sacred being and I thanked his mother for allowing me to touch them both and for his words of wisdom. The power of the words and the sorrow conveyed in them made me feel very sad at the stupidity of mankind and the way we had treated the planet and disrespected its inhabitants. I also reflected on how, in the western world, we had become separated from Mother Nature and the rhythms of the planets. We seemed to be on a downward spiral of only seeing what we could take rather than what we might give back. I prayed that with the return of these creatures, the tide would turn. It was time we changed our ways and started listening to the real guardians

The beautiful white buffalo at Flagstaff

of the planet. How arrogant to believe that we were the superior species.

It was with a mixture of awe, sadness and gratitude that we left the buffalo. The owner of the centre gave us a gift of a tuft of white buffalo fur from their shedding winter coats. I have kept that tuft and I sometimes feel it, just to tune into their energy and remind me of their message and how wonderful it was to gaze into their doleful dark eyes, and feel the soft sweep of air from the calf's breath as it caressed my hand.

We journeyed on to Kingman and Bullhead City, anchoring in more healing energy at various spots we felt drawn to. We felt some very negative energy in the area and there seemed to be a lot of extinct volcanic mounds in the landscape. I began to feel that at some time in the future, this would be an area that might suffer earthquake or flood, but I had a very uneasy feel about it, which was reinforced by a new guide that I had met before my journey. I was shown a huge feathered fan and it was being brandished by Quetzcoatl, the serpent headed Mayan god. I was to meet him again at my visit to Chitzen Itsa, but for now he seemed to be showing his discontent with the state of the planet and I saw him using the fan symbolically to obliterate certain areas around us. It made me shudder as it seemed to be a very real premonition.

We said goodbye to Nick and thanked him for driving us and being part of our ceremonies and rituals, and flew to San Jose via Salt Lake City. We were met by another of Magi's contacts, who was the sister of the lady who had had put us up in Sedona. She was a wonderful shaman and a joy to be around. She took us to the Rosicrucian Egyptian museum where there was a huge statue of Sekhmet. All of us were drawn to sit in front of the statue that was festooned with garlands and offerings of fruit and bread. It's so amazing that a stone statue can hold so much power and that the essence of the 'goddess' can be so encapsulated within it. The statues become alive with their overwhelming presence. This statue was no exception. We sat on the stone floor meditating and giving her our respect and it then felt like I had become a small lion cub, and Sekhmet, as a lioness, lifted me by the scruff with my tiny paws dangling. I then felt able to suckle her and I could feel a fiery glow as the lion milk flowed into my stomach. I was given the words:

"You have suckled from my breast and been filled with the fire of lion's milk, you must hold no fear from now on."

I then felt like I had been placed back on the floor in my cross-legged position. I opened my eyes, dazed at what had transpired, feeling the inner fire still within me. I wondered at the power a statue could have, remembering only too well the effect Sekhmet's stony presence had had on me in Egypt. It all seemed like yet more preparation for the future and healing of the past as I was finding my way back on my life's path.

The rest of our time was spent finding yet more areas for our ceremonies and we also visited a crystal fair at Quartzite. A large field seemed to be filled with stalls of every type of crystal imaginable. I had wanted to find a quartz point that could be used to make a wand that I had seen in one of the Egyptian visions which I painted. It showed a leonine head with the cobra ureaus and the sun disc. Next to the figure was large golden staff with a huge crystal at its tip with the inner fire of the light crystal energy. I searched the stalls, feeling quite overwhelmed with the all the power the different crystals were giving off and then I came to a stall selling Brazilian Quartz. I found just the right crystal, which seemed to bleep at me as I walked by and I asked it if it would be happy to be with me. I felt that it was okay with journeying back to England, so I bought it and it has now been made into a beautiful wand, respectfully joined to a wonderful piece of wood that came from mountains in Italy. I then searched and found Magi playing some beautiful crystal bowls and singing in angelic tones that drew a crowd of people to hear the magical sound.

Finally, it was time to fly home from what seemed like an all too brief stay in America, but I felt that we had packed so much into a short space of time. On the plane, I felt the buffalo hair and crystal that I had placed in my bag and reminisced about my recent adventures. Again I had felt very altered by everything I had experienced. I hoped that my contribution had played a small part in bringing some healing to the planet in whatever way was most appropriate. I looked forward to seeing my young son and the animals and to see what my next adventure would unfold.

The stone statue of Sekhmet, festooned with garlands and offerings of fruit and bread

The Rocky Mountains,
orca and bears

⁘

I have included this journey as it was the start of my connection with whales. I hope it illustrates that even though there are ups and downs in travelling, in my inexperienced way I 'muddled' through and had very valuable quality time with my youngest son. He has learnt to have such a great awareness of nature and the sacredness of the planet, which I feel started with this trip. Our children are the future and if we can raise their awareness of how precious all life is, they will hopefully be far better caretakers of the planet than their predecessors have been.

We had talked of riding on the Rocky Mountain railway for a number of years as my husband and youngest son loved everything to do with trains. Now that I was on my own, trying to support my son emotionally through the trauma of our divorce and all the losses that seemed to be incurred in our lives, I determined to take him on that journey myself, so that we could spend special time together and he could indulge his passion. His father and I had got married in Vancouver. I had fallen in love with Canada and I was so looking forward to returning, although with bittersweet memories of happier times there. One thing I felt had been kindled was a passion for large cetaceans, as we had visited the Marine science aquarium there and I had been transfixed by the spectacle of the two huge killer whales that were kept in a enormous aquarium with glass viewing panels and their sounds were amplified by hydrophones placed in the watery enclosure. I spent a long time pressed against the glass staring in wonder at the fabulous creatures swimming past me. Sometimes they came face to face with me, on occasion opening their mouths, so I could peep down into their throats. I felt sad that they should be confined to this life of captivity, but honoured to connect with them. This was all before my communication channels had been re-awakened, but I did fall in love with their energy, and came home with an orca mug and key ring – silly touristy mementos that I bought to somehow keep their connection and to continue thinking about them.

We landed in Calgary at the time of the stampede. Travelling on my own with a young child was still so new to me and it was a scary prospect, even just booking the holiday myself. As we entered the arrival lounge, the stampede mood was in full swing, and we were 'branded' with a pretend branding iron, welcoming us to Calgary. We were met by the tour representative and led to our bus transfer to the hotel.

After breakfast and a good night's sleep, we caught the bus to Canmore, where we took a helicopter ride over the Rockies. My son was lucky enough to sit in the front with the pilot and had a bird's eye view of the spectacular scenery. I was a little concerned as to whether it might be frightening, but we loved it! I thought that as we were here we might as well experience everything we could to make the most of our trip.

Our next stop was Banff, which was a very special place. We marvelled at the countryside as we travelled on the coach and kept an eye out for wildlife. My son seemed to have an uncanny knack of spotting creatures before anyone else and I discovered that he could 'feel' them before we could see them. I tested this as we walked around a beautiful lake and I felt the energy of a bear, not far away in the dense woods. I asked him if he could feel anything and were there any animals near? He said he thought there was a brown bear nearby and I asked him how he knew. He said that he could feel it in his tummy. I had the picture of a brown bear in my mind and I wondered if perhaps I had telepathically sent him the picture. However, the next time it happened I was distracted and he announced that he could 'feel' a black bear, somewhere in the wilderness around us. When I checked intuitively, I could also feel its energy. We never saw the bears, but we certainly 'felt' their presence as they wisely kept away from human interference. But on the bus when we saw the creatures, everyone was beginning to be a little surprised at our premonitions. I wanted to send the bears our love and apologize for invading their territory and prayed for them to keep safe. I placed some light crystals in the form of the etheric orbs which I hoped might bring some healing to the land.

We also visited Spirit Island, apparently so called as it was deemed to capture the spirit of Canada; it felt a very special place and I was also guided to place the crystals there. My favourite place was Moraine Lake. We scrambled up a rocky hill to be met with the most dazzling sight of shimmering turquoise water beneath us. We had also visited Lake Louise with its beautifully replicated reflections, and there was something about this lake that felt wild and free. I have decided that I would like my ashes scattered there as well as near my 'fairy tree'! We also visited the Athabasca Glacier on a huge wheeled vehicle and were told we had fifteen minutes to explore the icy terrain. We were quite downhearted at only having that short time, but after ten minutes all of us were beginning to feel the biting cold of the mighty 1000 feet thick glacier. We were clamouring to get back onto the bus as we struggled with the cold. I reflected on the enormity of the time the glacier had been in place there

Spirit Island, a very special place

as we cuddled together to keep warm. Sadly due to climate change, the glacier is receding far more rapidly than ever before.

We caught the Rocky Mountaineer train at Jasper and we also went on a river raft, and were warned to take towels as we were likely to get very wet backsides. I wondered how that would be possible as we were wrapped from head to toe in waterproofs. We took our places in the inflatable raft along with several other people and two dogs. The old dog, aptly named Jasper, sat in the centre of the raft and we wondered why until the young black labrador, who draped himself over the bow of the raft, got drenched as a wave from the rapids whooshed up and caught him right in the face. The old dog seemed to be chuckling as he kept at a safe distance from the water. Again we passed through some wonderful scenery and we clung to the sides of the raft as it whirled through the rapids. When we alighted from the raft we all had a rather shuffling gait as we became aware of our very soggy posteriors where the water had seeped in. Only Jasper the old dog seemed dry as he leapt onshore.

My son was so thrilled to finally be on the train and spent nearly the whole time hanging out of the corridor window taking photos of the fabulous scenery. I wondered at times why I had bothered paying for a seat for him, as he was rarely seated! I also loved the feeling of the gentle meandering train as we snaked through the passes and mountains, past waterfalls, rivers, over high bridges and through tunnels.

All too quickly we arrived in Vancouver, leaving behind the breathtaking sights and the long glass-topped train. It was very strange being back in the city. The last time I'd been there it had been so romantic, having our wedding and honeymoon on the spur of the moment. It was sad to see some of the sights we had seen together but under very different circumstances this time. I took my son back to the aquarium. They had re-homed the orca, but sadly I don't think they survived the move after so many years in their Vancouver home. We chatted to the Beluga whales who splashed the visitors as they erupted from their watery depths. I was still unhappy about the creatures being in captivity but hoped that the research carried out there was of benefit to both captive and wild cetaceans.

We booked our final trip to visit Victoria Island and a wild orca spotting boat excursion. We arrived at the jetty and were dressed in hooded boilersuit-type garments as we were told that it could get cold out on the water. I was very grateful for our extra clothing as we skimmed and bounced over the waves, shrieking with joy. We came upon a small pod of killer whales and we were told that a calf had just been born, as a small amount of placenta had been spotted in the water. We kept a respectful distance from the family, but the large male, probably the father of the calf, still wanted to hunt for fish. I was trying to photograph them in the water, but as I was staring through the lens, I was rather shocked to see the huge male coming straight for us as he lunged after the fish. I abandoned my camera as he averted his headlong rush at our small craft at the very last minute, narrowly missing capsizing us. He was magnificent and the

Beautiful colours reflected in Lake Louise

black markings on his body, gleamed in the sunlight. He had a slightly droopy dorsal fin, so was easily recognized by the boat captain. They had logged the identities of all the orca, so they could research their progress and population statistics. I decided to forgo taking any more pictures as I felt that it was spoiling my experience.

Instead, I just tuned into their energy and I felt such a rush of emotion for the family group. I felt they were very proud of their new arrival and seemed to have very strong family ties and affection for one another. It was like they were all connected by an invisible cord and although we couldn't hear their vocal exchanges we knew they were sensing each other's whereabouts constantly. We felt very privileged as we bobbed about on the waves and my son and I imagined sending out all our love to family and their new baby. I was so pleased to be able to share the experience with my son who was fast becoming more confident with his intuitive skills. The experience with him 'feeling' the bears reinforced my opinion that he was a very special child. Finally it was time to say goodbye to the whales. We wished them well and hoped their baby would thrive. On the ferry journey home we saw many more orca frolicking in the distant waves in that wonderful place.

The Azores and the Bahamas, dolphins and whales

I had dreamt of swimming with wild dolphins all my life and as my fiftieth birthday treat had to be postponed due to my mother's illness, my dream finally came true in 2005. I had searched the internet to find out about other dolphin trips that were not quite so far away, and found a trip advertized in the Azores, a small archipelago of islands in the Atlantic Ocean. About the time I booked the holiday, I had another session with my ex-naval officer and the strange Atlantean being came through via him again, and told me that I had to go to Mount Pico to perform a ceremony. I didn't know what exactly that entailed, but I felt that I would be 'told' when I got there. I had never heard of this mountain, but being a seafaring man he knew that one of the islands was called Pico Island, so I hoped that during our stay, we might be able to visit it. I was taking my son with me as I thought the interaction with dolphins might be healing for him. We had found that he had Aspergers Syndrome, so I hoped that the dolphin energy would help him become more confident in himself and expand his awareness of the planet.

We flew to Lisbon and then on to the tiny island of Faial. I had thought this was where our base was to be, but imagine my delight when I was told that we were catching the boat to another island – namely Pico Island. The large mountain we had seen from the plane as we came into land was indeed Mount Pico!

Having collected our bags, we searched for the representative who was to take us to the ferry and then collect the vehicle that would take us to our hotel. We scrambled onto the boat as our suitcases were unceremoniously tossed aboard, and together with the islanders and much needed produce, we started our journey across the waves to Pico Island. We were met by a lady who spoke no English and we were ushered onto a rather dilapidated minibus. There were some road blocks due to festival parades, so we thought we were taking a *slight* detour in order to find the small road that led to our hotel. After an hour and a half of circumnavigating the island by various routes, we were all beginning to become a little impatient, especially as our lady driver seemed to be getting more and more flustered and seemed to be at a loss as to how to get us to our destination! She had used so much fuel beetling around the countryside with her bewildered passengers that we then had to stop and refuel. Eventually she seemed to have a sudden inspiration and we finally climbed up a steep road and turned into the driveway of the hotel. We were so grateful to finally be shown our rooms and to have a meal. The hotel, Aldeia da Fonte, was beautifully constructed of stone and built right on the cliff edge, a factor that was going to play an important role in the location of other residents on the island, who made themselves known to us all through the night. It was quite humid, so we left the shutters and top half of a stable door open as were no fans or air conditioning. My son and I were just trying to settle down into our beds, when the most extraordinary commotion filled the room. What I can only describe as a demented 'Punch' sound from a Punch and Judy show seemed to clamour through the walls and that whatever 'it' was, it felt like 'it' would be joining us in our rooms very soon.

After a disturbed night of wondering what on earth the sound was and what it might belong to, and if it had entered our rooms would it have been dangerous, we went into the main part of the hotel for breakfast. We were all curious as to what had kept us all awake and what on earth could have made all that noise. We were told that there was a huge colony of shearwater birds, which nested on the cliffs. We were in their territory! We were to later see their diving prowess as they showed off their aerobatic hunting skills. However sometimes it seemed as though they were determined to nest in our bedrooms, as it sounded as though they were going to fly right inside our rooms with their deafening squawks.

We were given our itineraries and boat trip timetables and then were ushered to the pool to practice our snorkelling skills before we were allowed into the open water with the dolphins. I had attended a novice diving course several years before, but my young son had never tried, so we practiced swimming up and down the pool. I was so proud of my son as he struggled, but he persevered and became very proficient. I was fine in the calm pool but did not fare as well when we came to the ocean.

On the next morning, we were driven to the small harbour village of Lajes. This was formerly a whaling village. Fortunately the spotters that would spot the whales from the cliff top towers for hunting now spotted them for tourist whale-watching tours. However, the ominous slipway where the whales would have been dragged up to be butchered, remained, and I was given a horrible 'vision' of the whole slope streaming with blood. So much trauma remained there, where so many whales had been slaughtered. I visualized pouring white light down on the area and washing the blood away and sending love to those magnificent creatures who had lost their lives. Thank goodness things had changed in order to save the whales and also create income for the village, as people flocked to this very special migratory path, for such a diversity of cetaceans that could now pass safely through the waters. I hoped my visualization might have helped a little in releasing some of the past barbarism.

My son and I climbed aboard the small motor boat in our wetsuits with our masks, snorkels and fins at hand. We were very excited at the prospect of swimming with wild dolphins. In the distance a huge sperm whale and its calf breached and crashed down into the frothy waves. The sea was choppy as the weather deteriorated, but undeterred we gently entered the water to connect with a small pod of bottlenose dolphins. However after about five minutes the waves and current became much stronger and although we were trying to put our snorkelling skills to good use, the waves were swamping us and the salt water was pouring down into our snorkels, causing us to choke and splutter as we inhaled what should have been fresh air. Instead, we were struggling to breath any air at all. The captain decided to pull us all out immediately, which was a shame as none of us got a chance to really see the dolphins. We were doubly disappointed when we heard that the other group, who had gone to a quieter bay, had had the most marvellous interaction with a large group of playful dolphins. It was nice for one of the members as it was her birthday and what better way to spend your special day than with wild dolphins who choose to play with you. Our group, however, were a little downcast at our aborted trip.

We did have one brief encounter with a bottlenose dolphin who chose my son to swim up to and spent some time inspecting him. You could have tied his smile behind his head as he revelled in the dolphin's attention. I was so thrilled for him – perhaps the wonderful dolphin had chosen him because of his challenges and had sent some healing to him. He'd had such a horrible past year, I was so glad to be able to facilitate this interaction, and to have shared it with him.

Before we left, I had a dream about giving a light crystal orb to a dolphin, and after he took it in his mouth he swam down to the ocean floor with it. I was told that this was in order to place the crystal into the oceanic grid lines, which seem to run in a similar way to the golden grid around the outside of the planet that I'd been shown in my Egyptian vision. I was so excited at the prospect of meeting this special dolphin and being able to perform this task, but as the week went on we weren't getting very good encounters due to the weather. On one occasion, the water was so rough we never went in at all, though we were lucky enough to witness more whales breaching in the distance, a fantastic sight. We saw pods of spinner, common, spotted and risso dolphins, but none seemed to fulfil my mission. My son was having a wonderful time, which was great and the island itself was beautiful. I was amazed to see their hedges of hydrangea bushes coming into their pink and blue finery as they flowered. It was worth venturing inland to explore the island itself, as it was quite unique and of course the mountain, an extinct volcano, was spectacular. Eventually I had to give myself a good talking too! I finally realized that perhaps I had already performed my task in my dream state, and that the whole expectation was spoiling my experience of being in this wonderful place. So I decided to let go and just enjoy myself and although we never really had very close encounters, I did start to appreciate how blessed we were to be in such a wonderful place. I had booked an extra day on the trip, so that I could spend my birthday with the whales and dolphins and also visit Pico Mountain properly, as the Atlantean being had said that I must. But on the last trip with the rest of the group we were honoured by the spectacle of a super pod of bottlenose dolphins cavorting through the sea, right next to our boat. There must have been around three hundred of them, frolicking and leaping past us. It seemed like they were passing us for ages. We felt that perhaps they were saying goodbye to us, and we thanked them so much for blessing us with such an awesome sight that I'm sure none of us would ever forget.

So on the last day, as I bid farewell to most of the group, who had to make their way home to their various destinations around the world, I celebrated my birthday by booking a taxi ride up the mountain in the morning and a whale-watching trip in the afternoon. I wasn't sure what I was supposed to do once I got up the mountain, but I knew I would be guided. Apparently, to get to the top and into the crater, you needed climbing gear which I didn't have, so I asked the driver to go as far as possible and then we would climb as high as we could, in order to find the right spot to perform the ceremony. It was a beautiful day, and as the taxi driver finally stopped where the road ran out, we got out and started to climb. A lady from the group, who had decided to stay a little longer, had said that she wanted to come with us. She was a gentle soul and very interested in spiritual and planetary healing. I suddenly felt as though I was being led to a fairly flat grassy area on the side of the mountain. I had a bottle of water with me, and I felt the Atlantean being's energy all around me. I was told to 'prepare' the ground for the ritual, by spraying the water from my mouth over the ground, so I was guided to take a mouthful and spurt it out onto the ground. My son was horrified by what I was doing, but I apologized and said that I was being told to do it!

I was then told to create a beautiful pillar of golden light and with the help of the other lady, standing opposite me, we both held the energy of this immense etheric column of light. A huge chalcedony, crystal-like, blue orb travelled down and down as it appeared to pass deep inside the mountain, whose roots were in the ocean. I was told that this enormous orb was aligning the grids and its energy seemed to radiate out into the vast ocean all around us. It felt incredibly powerful and I prayed yet again that whatever it was that I had done, it would be of some small help to the planet. The Atlantean energy seemed to dissipate as we felt that our task was done, and we returned to the taxi that was waiting for us, no doubt wondering what this mad English woman was doing!

The afternoon's trip was such a treat and I finally felt that my fifty-one years of waiting had been worthwhile. Although this was not a snorkelling trip and we would have to remain on the boat, we were so blessed with the most amazing sights. The boat we boarded was a very fast rib and we sat astride our seats with our life jackets on, hanging on to the seat handles in front of us as we bounced through the waves. We were all of us elated at the experience and the chance to witness the sightings of some of the world's most incredible sea creatures. It seemed as though every time we thought we had seen all that we could and were about to leave, another fantastic encounter presented itself. One of the most spectacular was a large pod of common dolphins hunting a huge shoal of fish, creating a fish ball and then attacking them in a feeding frenzy, aided by hoards of diving shearwaters. This very spectacle, in sight of Mount Pico, had been filmed for documentaries and here it was, happening right in front of us. The dolphins lunged and plunged in the sea, attacking the poor fish that rushed together trying to protect themselves from all sides as the birds swooped down from above, diving down to incredible depths to snatch their prey. Eventually, the fish numbers decimated, the birds and dolphins dwindled away. We were all stunned at what we had just witnessed at such close hand, and were about to leave to return to the shore when suddenly we were joined by a pod of pilot whales. Their dark, bullet shaped bodies effortlessly glided through the water all around us. We were not allowed to approach any whales to within a distance of 25 yards, but if they came up to us, choosing to interact with us, this was deemed as non-invasive, so we were thrilled at their presence. One in particular seemed almost glued to the side of the boat just where I was sitting. I suddenly got the message "Give him the orb"! So I was guided to put my hand out, palm upwards, inviting the universe to place the etheric orb in my hand, so that I could pass it to the small whale. A beautiful smaller version of the pale blue orb that we had seen pass down the golden column was placed into my hand. I visualized placing the orb into the mouth of the whale as he looked up at me. His eye seemed to be reassuring me that this was real and happening right here, right now! As soon as I felt he had received the orb, he immediately dived. I watched him descend, deeper and deeper, until I could no longer see his dark shape disappearing into the depths of the ocean, but he seemed to give me a picture of him nuzzling the orb into the sand as it sank into the oceanic grid. I was so elated that at last, I had been able to perform my task and hoped that whatever healing that was meant to take place was helped in some small way by my efforts, aided by a very special whale! Fifty one years seemed a very short time to wait to be allowed the privilege of interacting with such fabulous creatures. I felt I'd had the best birthday anyone could have wished for and I thanked my mother so much for making it possible for my dream to come true.

The Bahamas

The next year I had booked to fulfil yet another dream, of swimming with humpback whales, but sadly, at the last minute, the boat had been discovered to be unseaworthy due to hurricane damage, and all other craft were fully booked. I was heartbroken. I'd just gone through a horrendously stressful house move, having to sell our marital home in the country, and the only thing that was keeping my spirits up was the thought of soon being with the whales. I was struggling with the change and the emotional rollercoaster that I'd been on.

The whale trip was organised by a new friend called Jackie. She was an English woman who had decided to follow her dream and go to America and then run trips to encounter wild cetaceans. She was so disappointed for all of us that the trip had to be postponed until the next year, when she'd managed to book another boat for us, but the thought of a whole year, waiting to escape the negative feelings of the new village I lived in really depressed me. Jackie suggested that we come on one of her dolphin trips to the Bahamas in the summer. I thought this would be great for my son and I. She assured me that the encounters were very frequent and the dolphins seemed to actively seek out their human visitors to play with them. So I booked two seats to Florida. I felt we would both benefit from some dolphin energy. Although my son was coping very well, his school life was challenging and I thought some more quality time together would help us both.

The plane out from Gatwick was delayed, and we arrived at Atlanta airport with little time to catch our connecting flight to Florida. Going through American customs took forever and we missed the flight by four minutes. I also didn't have Jackie's number to let her know what had happened as she was supposed to be meeting our plane. Luckily, the airline took pity on us and allowed us to catch a later plane. I managed to find Jackie's number and let her know just before she was due to leave to collect us. Unfortunately it meant that we would arrive very late and I apologized for the unsocial hour of our estimated arrival. However we had to perform another sprint through the airport, as we found we had been waiting at the wrong departure gate. It had been changed without much notice, so several of us made the dash to the new gate, just in time to be admitted onto the plane. Missing one flight was annoying; missing two would have been just careless! Finally we arrived, dishevelled and exhausted, to be met by Jackie's smiley face, as she kindly drove us back to her home as West Palm Beach. Even in the dark, seeing the lights and the palm trees lifted my spirits and reminded me of my beloved Egypt.

We spent a couple of days with Jackie where we practiced our snorkelling skills. I remember holding my son's hand in the sea as we gazed down at the beautiful multicoloured parrot fish, nibbling away with their bird-like 'beaks'. There were so many lovely fish as we stared in wonder, wide-eyed in our masks. I shall never forget the sharing of that moment with him. There are times when it can be a very simple pleasure, like a lovely walk or a fabulous sunset, times that are all too brief, but you know that the moment was special, and those memories stay with you forever.

We smiled at each other when we saw the name of the little boat that was going to be our home for the next week out in the ocean. It was called "The Shearwater" and owned by Jim Abernathy. The boat was used by film crews and photographers who made documentaries about sharks and underwater adventures, so he was very experienced in finding the best places to see dolphins. I shall never forget the sight of the most perfect water I had ever seen, the very first morning we stepped out on deck after our night trip from West Palm Beach out into the Bahamian waters. The turquoise water was so crystal clear, the white sand on the ocean floor sparkled up at us, and we understood how the area got its name of 'White Sand Ridge'. It seemed that every day would bring yet more delights as we encountered friendly spotted dolphins that were only too happy to frolic and play around us. We tried our hands at diving on a small wreck called the Sugar Wreck. Sea life had taken over the ancient bones of the ship and wonderful corals and plants now inhabited its watery grave. The colours of the plants and the fish were wonderful. I remembered watching films about reefs and underwater life, but never thought that the colours could be that incredible in reality, but here we were swimming around in this fantastic place, dazzled by the multicoloured hues. The joy of just snorkelling in shallow water, just focusing on a tiny square foot of ocean floor, brought so many wonders as we studied the diversity of life that inhabited that little patch of our planet. We stared at a flounder who,

chameleon-like, changed colour as he swam across different surfaces. I learned new names like 'Juvenile Angel' fish, with their electric blue colour entrancing us as they swum in and out of the coral. I could have spent hours just staring down in wonder at the microcosms of activity that continued day in day out. I prayed that man could stop destroying this fragile planet. Mother Nature is so precious and seeing that tiny speck of the ocean that we pollute and desecrate so thoughtlessly made me ashamed to be part of the human race.

On another day, my son and I were blessed to have a wonderful encounter with a mother dolphin and her calf. The calf was so inquisitive and wanted to come and play with us, but his mother was trying to divert him away. We had been told that dolphins like to hear you sing underwater, so we did our best to emit soothing sounds which seem to work, as the mother relaxed and let the baby come to us. We had been

Beautiful dolphins swimming in the clear waters of White Sand Ridge

told never to touch the dolphins, as that would be far too invasive, but if they seemed to want to interact with us we could try opening our eyes as wide as possible in our masks as this seemed to interest them. So we practiced our wide-eyed expressions, staring out from inside our masks. The baby loved this and cavorted around us. The mother seemed much calmer and I telepathically told her what a beautiful baby she had, and thanked her so much for letting him swim with us. I bobbed my head up and down in the water, as the baby was swimming by. It charged around us and then stopped right in front of my face and nodded up and down, imitating my movements. I looked at my son underwater, and he was grinning from ear to ear at the baby's antics. It was quite difficult not to suck in sea water as we laughed at the beautiful being that had chosen to play with us. It was such a special interaction for us. The dolphins stayed with us for about 20 minutes and then just as suddenly disappeared.

Another wonderful experience that we will never forget was a night swim with the dolphins. We had just dried ourselves and were thinking about food, when Jim announced that he was going to shine the lights on the water to see if the dolphins would come and feed on the squid that would be attracted by the lights. We were warned that if the dolphin suddenly disappeared, we should get back on the boat as quickly as possible, as it might mean that sharks were in the area! As we stepped out into the water, it seemed very strange that away from the lights there was a nothingness. The dolphins rushed in, hunting the squid, leaping and charging all around us. We could feel their sonar clicking through our bodies, checking our presence and whereabouts and so they could gauge exactly where we were, as they burst up in front of us and at times right behind us. For short fragments of time, I pretended I was part of the pod, spiralling with them, in formation, as they raced through the water. It was an amazing experience to feel so much part of their energy. It was fantastic gazing down into the deep and seeing them rising like torpedoes, right up next to us. My son and I stayed in the water for about two hours, absolutely enthralled with being part of such an incredible

spectacle. The dolphins seemed to lose interest in the poor squid – or maybe they'd had their fill, so we climbed back on the boat, only to be told to quickly go to the bow of the boat as there were dolphins bow riding. What was so wonderful, were the spectacular lights of the bio luminescence that sparkled and sprayed off their emblazoned bodies as they crashed through the water. It was almost as though they were dragging thousands of fairy lights after them. We were so lucky to share that experience with the dolphins, as the conditions were rarely that good. It was wonderful to be out in the middle of the ocean away from the turmoil of modern life, and to be allowed to share that space with such incredible creatures.

The next morning as I lay on my bunk, my son suddenly rushed into the cabin and said, "Quick get up, they're shark wrangling!" I wasn't sure what he was talking about, but I grabbed some clothes and went up on deck. One of the crew members had a grouper's head on a rope and he had been trailing it in the water and had been 'chumming' fish entrails and blood to attract the sharks. We seemed to be surrounded by enormous sharks. Tiger sharks are fierce looking creatures, lemon sharks slightly less so, but seeing them biting the fish head as they rolled their black eyes and exposed rows of needle teeth, I marvelled at their perfection. They are magnificent, beautiful, awesome and terrifying predators, and have been that way for millions of years, and we massacre them in their thousands, just for their fins or for so-called 'sport'. The largest tiger shark, named Tanya, had been encountered on several occasions. Her striped, lithe body cut through the water like a hot knife as she lunged at the fish and tugged on the rope that the crew member struggled to hold with the force of her attack. There was a small, tailgate-like affair called a 'swim step', where divers can step off the boat into the sea. One of our party, an American girl, was kneeling with her camera on the step in order to get some shots of the shark, half in and half out of the water, as it bit the fish head tied to the rope. All of a sudden, the American girl leapt into the air and landed back on the deck, looking white as a sheet –

Tanya had decided to launch herself onto the swim step! She bit through the rope and chewed the chains that held the step in place. We were all shocked at this! Eventually she wriggled off, unharmed, with a huge splash. I later tuned in to the sharks and thanked them for their presence. I felt they had much to teach us about adapting to the environment and how brilliant Mother Nature was to create their perfect design. We need to respect and protect these perfect creatures so that they can exist for many more thousands of years.

Stark warnings from the sharks

"Listen and Listen well! Why do you assume you are the superior species on the earth? Why then are you so fearful of us? Our perfect form requires no modification and has been that way for eons of time. But you destroy us and our habitat, through fear and petty gain. If you take it upon yourselves to change the balance of Mother Nature, you will destroy the balance for yourselves. Every microcosm has its part to play and if you remove just one link of nature's chain, there will be consequences. As you dishonour us, you dishonour yourselves. The more detached you become from the needs of the planet, the further you stray from your path. There was a time when you worked with the earth and not against it, that time must come again."
—Message from the lemon and tiger sharks of the Bahamas

We had many more wonderful encounters with our dolphin friends and swam amongst huge shoals of yellow finned jacks, in that incredibly clear water. We made new friends and our hearts filled with memories of that special place. We were all sad to return to land and our busy lives, which had been put on hold while we lived away on the ocean. I hoped the messages I had been given could be conveyed to alert mankind to the dangers of tampering with our Earth's perfect natural balance.

We will always remember our special time with the dolphins

Oceans of love from the humpbacks

I remember seeing some leaflets at a workshop one day advertizing a spiritual journey with humpbacks. The cost of the trip was too much at the time, but I remember thinking that it would be so amazing to actually swim in the ocean with a whale. I dismissed the possibility from my mind until one day after my mother had passed and I had met Magi. She telephoned me and asked if I might accommodate a friend of hers who was coming up to Glastonbury to attend a ceremony, which I was also going to. This lovely lady had MS, so Magi thought it would be a good idea if I collected her from the railway station and put her up for the night, and then drive her to the venue the next day. I was very happy to do this and afterwards marvelled at the way the universe sets things in motion when you least expect it!

When we were happily installed back at my house and drinking a cup of tea, I noticed that she was wearing a beautiful silver pendant of a whale's tail or fluke. I commented on it and she said she had been lucky enough to swim with humpback whales the year before, and that it was a treasured possession that she felt was a gift from the whales. My curiosity was immediately aroused, and the memory of those flyers advertizing the spiritual journeys from about two years previously popped into my head. I quizzed her on who ran these trips and dared to ask the cost. Although it was still a lot of money, it was a lot less that the other trips, so I asked if she might give me the details of the person who ran these adventures. This of course was Jackie who, as I mentioned earlier, had her own business called Wild Ocean Adventures. I have since travelled many times with her. Having enough money in my 'adventure fund', I decided to book the trip straight away as it really was the chance of a lifetime!

So, a year later, I landed at Puerto Plata in the Dominican Republic.

In the airport, we saw huge posters advertizing the new oceanarium that had just been completed. It boasted dolphin displays and invited you to come and swim with them. I immediately thought that was one place I would definitely *not* be visiting, as I hated the idea of captive dolphins, having seen them in their rightful environment in the wild. However the dolphins had other plans for me!

I had asked for a quiet room in the large hotel complex, where I was to stay for a few days before we caught the motor yacht that was to be our home on the ocean for a week with the whales. On the transfer bus I made myself known to Caroline, who was going to be joining us as a 70th birthday present to herself. However when we arrived at the hotel, they placed me in a huge suite and Caroline in a tiny room at the other end of the hotel complex. I'd asked if I could have a room near her and they said that they were full. I plucked up courage and asked the hotel manager if there was another room that I could have, and I was moved across the hall to a smaller room. It was a great improvement, that is, until night-time. The karaoke started at about 10pm when I discovered that my room was right next door, and this went on till about three o'clock in the morning. Finally the music died down and I started to drift in and out of sleep, when I felt I was joined by some very worried dolphins in my sleepy state.

They were from the oceanarium and were asking me to go there and help one of the other dolphins called Mani. They showed me her swimming in a very unbalanced way, rather like my pet goldfish when it had a problem with its swim bladder. I had been so sure that I didn't want to go to the oceanarium because of the captive state of the dolphins. I was certainly in no rush to patronize such a place and condone the practice of dolphin 'entertainment'. However, I could feel that I would not be allowed any rest until I promised to go to see them as soon as I could, in order to help their friend. So the next morning, when I told Caroline what had happened, we sought out the hotel rep and booked a trip to the oceanarium later that morning.

When Caroline and I arrived, our hearts sank as we heard the loud speakers jubilantly announcing the dolphin 'shows'. The first 'performance' was just starting and I watched with tears pouring down my face. We watched the dolphins doing their tricks, their beautiful bodies gleaming in the sunlight as they leapt into the air. Members of the public were allowed to hold onto their dorsal fins, so the dolphins could drag them through the water. I was so disgusted that they should be so degraded, by having to perform for us. (I feel even more disgusted now, having watched the film "The Cove", which shows how dolphins are captured in the wild in Japan to be selected for these sea worlds, and then the slaughter of those left behind. I'm sure that if more people watched the film, they would not show patronage to these places.) Please see how you can support them in the resource section at the end of this book.

I was ashamed to be there, but I knew the dolphins wanted my help. These beautiful ocean creatures should be wild and free and we wished that more people could witness their joy and playfulness in their natural habitat, where they have the choice to be with humans... or not! It is such a privilege to connect with a wild creature that chooses to interact with you. Caroline and I knew we'd been very lucky to have had this experience. She asked me how we were going to find Mani and I only knew that we would be guided by her dolphin friends, so we could give her the help she needed. There were several groups of dolphins in different pools, so we decided that we might choose an option where we could just sit in the pool and meet the dolphins. This seemed slightly less invasive, though they were encouraged to connect with us with buckets of fish to 'bribe' them to get close to people. There were only two dolphins working in this way as we took our positions in the pool. One of the dolphins had a baby that was kept separate from us. As she swam past me, I just knew it was Mani. The keeper called her Serena. I prayed that I was right and that I could be of help to her. The dolphins were taught to splash us and shake fins and then come right up to us and lean on our shoulders. As soon as Mani leaned on my shoulder, I felt her physical and emotional pain.

I held her as gently as I could, pouring as much love and healing energy into her beautiful body. I desperately hoped that our short encounter had helped in some way. Photos were taken of our encounters, and as we left, I brought back the photo of Mani and I, and it became the cover for my first book, *An Exchange of Love*. I also hoped that if I had a photo of her I might be able to continue sending her healing, if I could. I wanted to share the importance of the roles these creatures play in our lives.

That night I lay in bed thinking about the day's events. I tried to remember the amazing feeling of Mani's energy as she laid in my arms – the texture of her cool skin and the strength in her beautiful body. All of a sudden, to my total surprise, I felt the weight of her presence on my shoulder once again, as though she wanted to give me more information. I couldn't believe it as it felt so real, and she communicated that she was so sad because her baby would never be free. She seemed frustrated that she felt so disconnected from her soul origins, and what she called 'source' – the universal connection to all that is and the absolute knowing that all is one. Her captivity had imprisoned her physically and spiritually. I visualized giving her healing in the normal way that the animals had taught me, by imagining placing my hand on her tail and sending energy up through her body. This facilitated a balancing of her chakra systems, but to my amazement she told me that although the positions of her physical chakras were similar to ours, she had 12 higher soul chakras and that the whales had 21! These chakras, she explained, were linked to the planetary grids, which is why the cetaceans were so important to the planet. As I worked to rebalance her, thanking her for the gifts of her insights, I realized she was preparing me for my encounters with the whales, which I was to experience in the next couple of days. I felt she had become disconnected because of her distress for her baby. I realized that she could escape from her captivity if she just detached from her fear. We 'discussed' the potential of astral travel and bi-location, and that really she could 'journey' anywhere she wanted to, outside of her physical body, and that she could teach this to her baby. She seemed much more at peace, which made me so happy. And then she was gone. I drifted off to sleep and then became aware of her energetic presence again, in the early hours of the morning. I felt her gentle pressure on my right shoulder and then the most incredible waves of almost electric energy pulsating through my body. I began to shudder as it was so powerful, and felt she was reciprocating, with a healing exchange. The power of what was happening to me was incredible and I shall never forget it.

Meeting Caroline the next morning, I told her what had happened; we reflected that maybe these special dolphins were performing a much deeper role in reaching the masses in their captive state. Many more people would interact with dolphins in these awful places, but maybe they would be affected by the dolphin energy, which would re-awaken a deep awareness. Having met the Indian elephants that I recall in a later chapter, I realized that many creatures are such brave souls, which commit to contracting very challenging incarnations, as do us humans. Unfortunately as we get bogged down by those challenges, we don't always remember their purpose, and the importance of those roles to teach others—yet more evidence of just how amazing our animal friends are.

Meeting the humpbacks

Words alone cannot describe the enormity of the presence of a whale as you swim next to it. Living out on the ocean surrounded by them for a week was such a profound experience that was to alter my life forever. To be able to connect with the caretakers of the planet in such trusting proximity is a blessing beyond words. The sheer size and power of their energy is almost impossible to describe. I thought that connecting with Mani had been powerful, but nothing compared to the beings I was about to encounter next!

Finally the day came when we would leave the Dominican Republic and sail out into the ocean. We were all so excited at the prospect of meeting the whales. We boarded our boat from the dock in Puerto Plata and I was to share my cabin with a lovely American lady. It was odd sharing such a small space with a complete stranger, but we soon got tucked up in our bunks and fell asleep to the sound of the engine and the rise and fall of the waves.

We travelled about eight hours out into the ocean to an area called the Silver Banks, in between the Dominican Republic and the Turks and Caicos islands. This area is chosen by the female whales because it seems to be a safe area for calving, and for the males to find their new mates. There can be as many as 150 whales in the area at any time, so being immersed in all that energy for a whole week was incredible!

We awoke to the smell of breakfast and the prospect of our first encounter. There were, however, some other smells which were not so inviting. Toilets on a boat are called 'heads' and an inconsiderate previous guest had managed to block one of ours. The crew were desperately trying to resolve the problem, and at one stage only one toilet on the boat worked. However the excitement of the first trip out to meet the whales and actually swim with them overrode everything else. We had been shown videos on etiquette and respectful non-invasive encounters, especially with mothers and newborn calves. We were to board a small inflatable rib, which seemed very flimsy with huge 40 foot leviathans just beneath us. We could be capsized without them really even noticing! The whales of course were very gentle and aware of our presence. The company that had brought us here were very respectful of the whale's needs, and endeavoured to be as unobtrusive as possible. They only allowed people to enter the water when they were totally satisfied that the whales were relaxed and unconcerned with human presence.

I shall never forget the first trip where we all scrambled rather gingerly into the small boat. I had poured myself into my wetsuit with difficulty, as I had a frozen shoulder and anyone who has ever worn a wetsuit, will know of the contortions you have to perform in order to get in and out of it.

We waited in anticipation for our first sighting. Several members of our party were experienced underwater photographers and they prepared their cameras for the anticipated shots. We had not ventured very far out into the ocean away from the ship when I noticed a pale blue shape beneath us. It was a large pectoral fin of a whale right under us! We were told to sit still as the whale could come up right beneath us and tip the boat over. We felt the whale touch the underside of the boat and then gently dive a little lower in the water and then surface right in front of us. Its wonderful blowhole sucked in air and blew out its spray. It was the most amazing sound and we were all mesmerized. We were actually sitting in a boat with a 40 foot whale right next to us. Others were surfacing only a few yards away. Seeing these leviathans surfacing and breaching and blowing right next to us was just sublime. The captain waited to see if the whale was happy with our presence, and when he was satisfied that the whale didn't feel threatened by us, he instructed us on how to enter the water without disturbing it and to gently swim towards it. If the whale decided to swim away we were not allowed to pursue it and most definitely not touch it. I gently slid down the side of the inflatable rib and felt the cool water seep into my wetsuit. The whale allowed us to approach, watching us with its wonderfully wise eye. Looking into the eye of a whale is something beyond description and is one of the greatest experiences of my life. Once again I felt incredibly blessed. The whale decided to depart, so thanking him with all my heart we watched him swish his huge fluke as it propelled him effortlessly through the water and out of sight. I had to be lifted out rather unceremoniously, as I found it hard to pull myself up with my weakened shoulder. This was even more embarrassing one day, when a mother and calf swam alongside the big boat, when we had all just got dry and dressed ready for lunch. I had pulled on a white tee shirt and pale thin cotton trousers. We were told to just grab our masks and jump in, in order to swim with them. Without thinking, I did as I was instructed and jumped in fully clothed into the water. The mother was quite relaxed but guided her baby away after a few minutes. I had to be lifted out again, but suddenly realized why everyone seemed to find this very amusing.

I looked down at my dripping body and realized that I would have made a good candidate for a wet tee-shirt competition!

We had many incredible encounters. Occasionally, several males would compete for female attention and they would have battles by fin or tail slapping, which was quite a display. One time, I was treading water with my fins when I saw, coming towards us at speed, four males or 'rowdies'. This was worrying, as they could have seriously injured us as they battled with their titanic rivals. However they halted their aggression and just dived down beneath us. I watched in silent amazement as one by one the rivals propelled themselves beneath us. Once safely distanced from us they resumed their wonderful displays of fin and fluke slapping.

On another occasion, a juvenile male appeared to be hovering, nose down in the water. I swam closer, feeling that he was relaxed with my presence, and sent out lots of love from my heart, thanking him for allowing me to be near. He seemed fairly oblivious, and was singing in incredibly deep tones that seemed to rattle and vibrate through my body. I could feel it affecting me physiologically, as my body seemed to resonate with the glorious but mournful sounds. However I was not so calm when I realized that he had completed his sad serenade and was about to surface right beneath me. I knew that I was not going to be able to get out of his way in time, so I was not a little alarmed! I felt that he might have a new passenger, however unwittingly. However he was obviously totally aware of my dimensions and determined exactly how close he could come without harming me. He remained quite level – almost flat about a foot beneath me, and only came up in the telltale 'hump' shape of his back once he was safely in front of me. His huge tail fluke seemed only inches from my face! I thanked him for being so gentle with me and for allowing me to listen and witness his song. I prayed that he would one day find his mate and have safe passage on his migrations.

I had doubted that this experience could be topped but I was yet to meet the most important being, and as I have later realized, the catalyst for this book and my future work.

Gina

"You are not just a drop in the ocean.
You are the mighty ocean in the drop." —Rumi

On the third day of our journey with the whales, having split into two groups so that we could safely fit into the small ribs, we were contacted by the other rib's radio. A message came through that they had found a lovely mother and calf who seemed really content with human presence and apparently set to rest up for a while. She had seemed very happy to spend time with people, so we had been invited over to share the beautiful encounter. We sped through the waves with high anticipation to find them. As we gently lowered ourselves into the water I could see that the mother was enormous, she had barnacles attached to her tail and seemed such a wise ancient being. Her calf was about three weeks old and the mother appeared to be resting as the calf frolicked in the water. It was so curious to learn what these strange black creatures were and it seemed to be agog at our masked faces and snorkels. It kept circling us, examining us, looking straight into our eyes. As I said before, the sight of a whale's eye right next to you is something you could never forget. This baby continued its inspection of its strange visitors in such a nonchalant fashion, only being interrupted by its need to feed and take air. Its mother showed such immense trust in allowing us to interact with her baby for four hours, as we took it in turns to snorkel with them. We didn't have to swim so much as just hover, floating in the calm sea, witnessing the glorious spectacle of her surfacing every 25 minutes or so. She would remind the calf by gently pushing him up with her huge pectoral fin to breathe at intervals of about six minutes. It would take a gulp of air and then perform a further inspection of our group, have some milk from his mother and then bob up to the surface, leaving a trail of milky fluid behind him. Then return for another stare! The water was so clear and the sunlight magically dappled the whale's skin as it shone down through the water. Everyone was busy taking photographs, some of which my Swiss friend Urs was kind enough to give me as a permanent record of this incredible experience. When I later printed out the pictures of the calf, the most beautiful rose quartz coloured orbs appeared all around him. We were so blessed to be imbued with the loving energy that flowed from this beautiful being, not only to us, but also the ocean.

Being in the middle of the ocean, floating right next to a humpback whale, looking at each other, as the whale gazes into your eyes, is so awe-inspiring, it's almost too much to grasp. I had to keep reminding myself that it was actually happening. This was a real whale's eye that I was staring into as it gently cruised by, or rested right next to me. I think it was such an overload of delight and awe at their magnificence that I found it difficult to tune into their wisdom whilst swimming next to them. However, when I was in my bunk at night I felt their presence pervade the cabin and I busily scribbled down the conversations! The whales could be heard blowing all around the boat at night, making their wonderful sounds as they surfaced. If you were on deck it was hard to keep up with their appearances as they would appear, first on one side of the boat, and then the next. We ran to port and starboard so many times, so as not to miss the chance to view the beautiful creatures and drink in their energy that we were being immersed in.

Planetary healing with whale wisdom

Before I'd left on my trip of a lifetime, I'd been contacted by a network of healers who were synchronizing a global healing event to take place on a day when I would be with the whales. The purpose of the healing was to anchor in the Divine Lotus Heart energy. We were to unite on that particular day across the time zones, to work to bring that beautiful energy to the planet. I told them I would be with the humpbacks at that

Photographing Gina with her calf

time and what better co-creators of healing energy than the whales? I told the group that I would ask the whales permission to enlist their help.

The night before the day of collective healing, I decided to tune into the mother whale. I felt the enormity of her presence connect with my energy, the power of which made me shudder. I asked her if she had a name I could call her. Showing much tolerance, she gently told me to call her Gina. She told me that she knew how humans loved to name things so we could reconnect more easily with their energy. I thanked her from the depths of my being. I wanted to show my gratitude for allowing us to spend so much time with her and her precious baby.

Gina said that she wanted to teach us about *trust*, something that we had become very detached and disconnected from. I couldn't believe that this immense being was showing such compassion to a species that had singlehandedly nearly wiped out their presence on earth. She explained that it was essential that we believed in the deeper concept of trust – especially within ourselves. The outpouring of wisdom that followed had me wiping tears from my eyes, as I scribbled away with my pen.

I asked her if she would help us with the planetary healing and that perhaps she could guide me as to the best way to assist the global effort. I questioned her to see if she had any knowledge of the Lotus Heart. She told me that this cushions the planet and that we have to send as much love out to the planet and into ourselves, in order for the planet to be lowered into the protective divine love of the Lotus Heart. She advised me to visualize the earth being gently wrapped in the divinity and joy of the one love, symbolized by the lotus. I also wanted to question her about the Akashic records. I'd been told that the whales were the record keepers, and that they held the keys of all that is. She replied that each and every one of us held the keys to the knowledge of the Akashic records. She said that the key was held in my heart and the way to activate the key, was to send loving energy into my heart. She likened me to a tiny ant that seemed to be rushing around, directionless. She went on to say that I perceived that I was separate and without purpose. I had to remember that, although I was tiny, I was a vital component of the colony, or part of the whole. She said that I was working to protect and heal my 'hill'... or the earth. She reminded me of the huge strength of the miniscule ant. I had often felt useless and ineffectual and Gina endowed me with the wisdom to combine forces with the 'colony' and become as one.

Her compassionate words poured into my mind as I lay in bed that night. It was overwhelming that this beautiful sentient being had the grace and love to see mankind as some form of wayward teenager that only needed understanding and love to bring them back to balance and harmony and, in so doing, create harmony for the whole of Mother Earth. I thought about her words, comparing me to an ant and remembered that size for size it was capable of incredible feats of strength far beyond its diminutive stature. She was right in describing the way I had been feeling about myself. I'd been feeling isolated and disconnected from the whole, wondering what difference I could make to anything going on in the world. My former friends seemed to feel that I'd lost the plot. I felt tremendous love from the animals, but had failed to send love to myself. Gina's generosity of spirit had given me this gift and I felt very blessed.

Anchoring the healing heart

Next day, with the help of a few interested people on board, I invited them to visualize Gina's vision of sending love into the earth. I explained her guided message of healing for the planet. She had shown me the earth floating above an immense lotus flower with a million petals open in readiness to welcome the planet into its protection. We knew we had to visualize it gently lowering itself into the heart of the flower, as it became more and more filled with love. So when the time arrived when we might

Gina's calf close up

connect globally, we were out on the ocean surrounded by the love of the whales. We all focused on the planet descending right into the heart of the lotus to be wrapped in love.

I prayed that our combined global efforts would create healing and love for our planet. I sent out the biggest 'thank you' in a wave of gratitude to Gina and the rest of the whales and hoped that she might feel my love from her deep ocean abode.

Later that night I meditated again, calling in Gina's guidance once more. I was so excited to see a massive shift in the earth's energy, and ecstatic to see it enveloped within the petals. I felt certain that our healing intent had helped to make a shift. I hoped and prayed that the planet would feel that healing physically. Caroline had given me a book by Dawn Baumann Brunke called *Animal Voices*. It reinforced many of my opinions of the importance of the role animals played in healing the planet. When I had finished my meditation, I read another chapter of the book where a description of a discussion with an orca was featured. I was amazed to read that the orca had 'talked' about the whale's wish for mankind to learn about 'The Greater Love', and the importance of love. The book was published in 2002, several years before my encounter with Gina, proving that the whale collective consciousness knows exactly what we need to know in order to bring about planetary healing. Once again, I realize we're just playing catch up! The author described the feelings and images that the orca gave to her, with the sound of her energy like a booming tone that resonated through the earth, making her heart appear like a huge lotus which symbolized the greater love.

What is wonderful is that I now realize that every species of whale is sending out the same messages of love – what truly awesome divine beings they are!

More advice from Pillow

"Guilt compresses and constricts the capacity to move forwards.
It enslaves you and inhibits your freedom. It is sapping your spirit,
draining your divinity. Breathe deeply and let it go!"
—Message from Pillow in spirit

Finally, it was time to leave the whales and set sail for the Dominican Republic. It was so hard to say goodbye, but I knew that the memories would stay with me forever. When we returned to the hotel, I started to feel quite shaky and unwell. I was exhausted and felt bereft, being in the heavy energy of the island after being immersed in such powerful loving energies during my week with the whales. I started to feel sick and I really thought I was going to pass out, so I went to my room to rest. Suddenly huge waves of emotion poured through my body, as I lay on my bed. I wondered what on earth was happening to me, as I couldn't stop crying. As I lay there my lovely dog in spirit, Pillow, who had shown herself to me in Egypt, bounded into my thoughts as unexpectedly as before. As I lay there sobbing, I tried to express the depth of my sorrow at her traumatic passing. I told her how lovely she was and how terrible it was to lose her. She had died at such a young age and I couldn't believe she'd left me so soon. To which she replied in my mind:

"I never 'left' you; you didn't 'lose' me! I am always around to guide you. My purpose for incarnating was to help you evolve and our connection was only to be for a short time. It was enough to reawaken your awareness of the limitation of negative emotion. Humans must let go of their feelings of grief, guilt and separation. There is no death. Animals know that it is just another part of the cycle, she explained. Animals understand the rebirth of death. There is such a big picture to the deep connections between us; you have to remember to look at the reasons and timing for our re-connections and passing. Feelings of guilt eat away at your soul and detract from your purpose. There are no mistakes, nothing was

*your fault, it was only for you to learn and grow from the experience. Celebrate
our connection. All is as it should be, emotions are only damaging when they
remain stored within the body, limiting and controlling your self beliefs.
They are only thoughts and they can be changed."*

She was such a special being and I had been lucky enough to share
her short life. I asked again if she would return to me in another physical
form, but she said she hadn't decided yet, as she felt that she could do
more healing work in her form as pure energy. She felt she was free from
restrictions of time and space. This of course was still very emotional for
me, but I did feel comforted to know that her presence was near whenever
I needed to be reminded about my limiting negative emotions!

I'd really had some profound emotional experiences while lying
on my hotel bed, with visitations from dolphins and now my dog.
Fortunately on my return to the hotel, I had been moved to a 'quiet'
room next to Caroline, on the ground floor. That night, however, there
was a tremendous tropical storm! I awoke, having drifted off to the sound
of rain and wind beating on my window. I nonchalantly stepped out of
my bed only to find at least four inches of water covering my bare foot
and my suitcase doing a good impression of a boat as it floated above the
floor. Someone with a mop appeared and once the sun returned I hung
my damp possessions out to dry. I never knew quite how the water had
got into my bedroom, as it was on the ground floor! Again I reflected
on the symbolic connection of water to our emotions, as I'd felt very
emotional leaving the whales and during another profound reconnection
with Pillow.

We said our farewells to other members of our group travelling back
to their homes, saying goodbye to the swaying palm trees and the sea.
I dozed on the long journey home and filled my mind with images of
whale's eyes and dripping flukes as they majestically tilted in the air,
ready to plunge once again into the depths. Again I conjured up the
sensation on Mani pressing against my shoulder, as I had felt her that

night in my hotel room. I have to say that the smell of damp remained until I washed all my clothes and my suitcase was never quite the same, however it managed to be of service for a few more adventures until a rather unpleasant adventure in India... but that's another story!

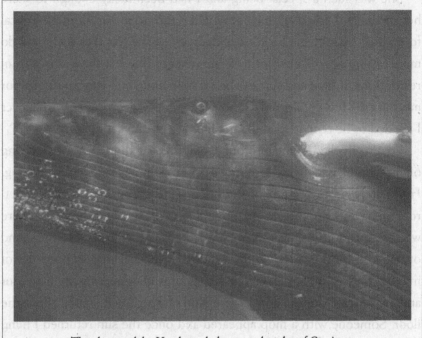

This photograph by Urs shows the beauty and wisdom of Gina's eye

The whale sharks and giant manta rays of Mexico

"Be the ambassador of yourself and manifest your heart's desire.
Every relationship teaches you more about yourself.
Where you've been and where you're going!"
—Whale shark Mexico 2008

I had watched a documentary on the television, where people were swimming alongside whale sharks. They had looked so tiny but had felt no fear from the gentle giants, as they cruised majestically through the water. I thought how incredible it would be to experience being in the water with that beautiful creature. When I was on the humpback trip, Jackie was discussing trying to put together a trip to Mexico to swim with the sharks. One of the captains, who was an avid underwater photographer, said that he'd heard the little island of Holbox off the Yucatan peninsula was the best place in the world to see the huge fish.

Jackie had set to work sourcing the right hotel and boat crew who would have integrity for non-invasive encounters and came up trumps with some dates for June 2007. It was to be a four day stay on the island, with three days of boat trips and then we could visit some Mayan sites back on the mainland if we wanted. I decided to book a week's trip and stay in Cancun and Chitzen Itsa, as I was fascinated by Mayan history. The person who I was to share a room with was coming from the Turks and Caicos Islands and so we agreed to meet at Cancun airport.

Mexico was so vibrant and full of colour, it had such a pulsating energy, and as I walked into the arrivals lounge my excitement grew. I spotted my future room-mate, Karen, waiting outside. She was an experienced diver,

*A beautiful
sunset from
the beach on
Holbox Island*

unlike me, but she said she was happy to be my snorkel buddy. I knew we were going to be great friends as we were both passionate about nature and animals. Finally, the others arrived and we piled into the minibus. A few people from the whale trip were there and it was great to meet them again and reminisce about the whales. I was exhausted after my long flight and wait at the airport, but we were all on such a high as we took our seats on the bustling boat filled with islanders and supplies. We craned our necks to see as much of the scenery as we could and then we spotted the island in front of us. Our excitement was at fever pitch as we knew we were about to arrive at the place that was to be our home for the next few days, and the best place in the world to encounter whale sharks.

The sun was beginning to set and we arrived at our idyllic hotel just in time for the sunset over the ocean and it was breathtaking. The hotel entrance was festooned with bougainvillea and fairy lights, coconut palms and banana trees. Karen and I were shown to our room that looked right out onto the ocean. We thought we'd found paradise. Even the bathroom was brightly decorated, with the shower water cascading from a conch shell. Hammocks stretched from the palm trees outside our room and the ocean beckoned us just a few yards away. We fell asleep to the sounds of the waves lapping on the shore and the gentle rustle of the wind in the palms. We had to be ready on the beach by seven o'clock the next morning to get our briefing from the captain of the small boat Jackie had hired for the duration.

We awoke to the sounds of the tropical birds serenading us from the palms and the azure blue sky, with the sun already beating down. We met our captain and guide, who spoke excellent English. He wrapped wrist bands on us and told us about what we might expect and how to behave in order to respect the sharks. They were part of a research team who identify each whale shark they encounter so they can check on the welfare of the population and migratory paths. We were given briefings of the research work and the behaviour of the sharks. We sailed for about an hour and a half and then the boat slowed and the guide beckoned me up to the bow of the boat where I got my first sight of a whale shark, cutting through the emerald green water. I could see its spotted head peeping up and then several feet back a dorsal fin and then what seemed like forever, a tail fin gliding behind. It was obviously a very large creature as its body seemed to go on and on as it passed our boat. We decided who was going to go in first as we were allowed to enter the water in pairs with the guide helping us and indentifying each shark we encountered. I shall never forget the first time I clutched onto the side of the boat with my legs and fins dangling into the water as we skimmed along. I'd struggled to get my mask fitting properly and my snorkel was shoved in my mouth as I tried to remember everything I'd been taught about gentle entry. I also primed myself about blowing out any water that came into my snorkel, so that I wouldn't inhale sea water. Karen was much more experienced and waited patiently for the order to 'go'! The boat circled and we were perfectly placed to meet our first whale shark. My heart leapt in my mouth as I heard the captain shout his order. Holding the side of the boat, I tried to slip into the water with the least amount of disturbance, as we didn't want to frighten or upset the shark. I almost shrieked as I found myself right in front of an enormous shark coming straight towards me with its

Sunlight reflecting through the water onto a dappled whale shark

mouth wide open, feeding on plankton that was rich in the waters at that time of the year. I felt rooted to the spot and was mesmerized as the huge creature gently closed its mouth – I had felt it might swallow me as it was enormous. The shark looked quizzically at me with its tiny eye, not in the least worried by my presence. Its massive gills billowed in the water and the sun dappled its immense spotted back. I tried to send waves of love out from my heart, as I thanked the fish for allowing me to join it in the water. Our guide had free-dived beneath the shark to determine its sex and whether it had been tagged, and he was able to identify it as a male that had swum in the waters for several years. Although I had been a little scared at first at the sheer size of the creature, I realized that I was in no danger and that I had been so privileged to be accepted by this fantastic being. As I stumbled up the small ladder trying to remove my fins, I think my expression said it all. I'd had such an incredible experience. We all had wonderful encounters and at one stage there were about six sharks feeding around the boat. Jackie said that she had spent two weeks in Australia and had only seen one shark on the whole trip. This was phenomenal and we were so lucky to see so many sharks on our very first morning. The crew seemed just as excited as we were and shared our emotional experiences as we hauled ourselves dripping back into the boat. We finally had to leave the ocean to return to shore and I visualized dropping light crystals into the watery depths, hoping it would bring some healing energy to the ocean.

The next days were just as wonderful with so many fantastic encounters; we loved the island and its watery neighbours. We met a couple of manta rays who were a little shy, so we refrained from pursuing them and I silently thanked them for showing us their beauty as they 'flew' through the water. We also nearly bumped into a mating pair of turtles who bobbed up and down in the waves. They seemed most perturbed at our invasion of their privacy and we quickly sailed past them leaving them to their romantic liaison. On my last encounter, I met a fairly young shark who was about 30 feet long and very docile, so I had no difficulty keeping up with him as I finned along, trying to keep in his slip stream next to his large gills and beautiful piercing eye. He almost seemed to be dawdling as I had found it quite hard to keep up with others I had swum with. It was deceptive from the surface looking down on the giant fish that hardly seemed to be moving. In the water, however, their tails were such powerful propellers that one powerful swish could send the fish jetting away into the distance leaving us almost treading water. This fish, though, seemed to just float alongside me. I began to get some images in my mind that appeared to be coming from him. My mind was being filled with the picture of the Mayan pyramid at Chitzen Itsa. I was very surprised as you can imagine as it was the last thing I expected coming from a whale shark in the middle of the ocean. He 'said' in my mind that when I went and stood in front of the pyramid he would give me more instructions as to how to implement light crystal healing that would connect that pyramid with others around the world, to aid planetary union. My amazement grew at this unexpected interaction and dialogue. I thanked him so much for his message and, rather like

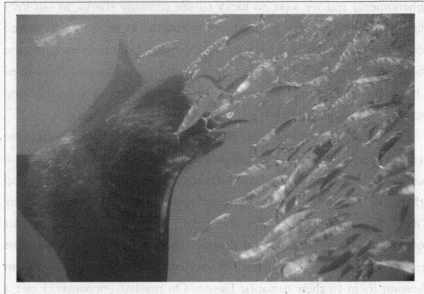

The magnificent manta ray swimming with a shoal of fish

Gina the whale, said I could call him Sonny, as though he also knew us humans liked to 'name' things! When it seemed that I had received and understood his message, he gave me one last intense stare and then gave a huge swish of his tail and shot off into the distance, becoming instantly lost in the vastness of the ocean. I was left feeling rather stunned at being 'spoken' to by a whale shark, especially as it seemed such a profound message. I couldn't wait to get to the ancient site to see what happened, but none of us really wanted to leave our island paradise. However, the weather, which had been blisteringly hot, suddenly deteriorated. A storm was brewing, so our captain wisely decided to take us back to shore. As we sped through the waves in the sea that was becoming increasingly choppy, I hoped our little boat would get us safely back. Thunder and lightning crashed all around us as the storm broke. The rain lashed down and I was just a little concerned at our metal mast that protruded upwards into the sky. We stopped at a small rocky outcrop at the far end of the island where there was a lighthouse and sheltered from the storm. We were all feeling the cold as the rain had soaked us to the skin. I comforted myself with the fact that the whale shark obviously believed I was going to get to Chitzen Itsa, so I should not be fearful and that we would be safe from harm. The storm abated and of course we reached the shore just as the sun peeped out from the black clouds, which disappeared as suddenly as they had arrived. We had one last evening of fabulous food and merriment at a restaurant we had found in the town, and we shopped for souvenirs on the way back to the hotel. We stepped through the gaily lit entrance and gazed out for one last time at the moonlit sea, eventually forcing ourselves to retire to bed.

We were all down-hearted at saying goodbye to our island paradise, as we loaded the golf carts with our cases, trundling past the now familiar shops and houses and back to the jetty to catch the ferry. It was the most magical place and we all agreed that if we could, we would come back one day soon. Some of the group flew home, but Karen, Alex, an American, and I, all wanted to visit Chitzen Itsa, so we took a taxi. Again we thirsted to absorb as much of the scenery as possible, to remember every aspect of this fantastic adventure into paradise. Rather like watching a tennis match, we glanced left and right out of the windows to witness the sights of rural Mexico as we drove through villages and dense jungle. It was easy to imagine how ancient sites could get swallowed up by the jungle, reclaiming its territory and concealing the secrets and mysteries of those forgotten times.

Eventually we turned into what seemed like a jungle track and were surprised to arrive at a beautiful modern hotel, where peacocks strutted around the grounds and dragon-like iguanas eyed us suspiciously. We decided to go to the sound and light show that was scheduled for that evening. It was really spectacular, as we had our first glimpse of the iconic pyramid and other parts of the complex lit with coloured lights and were told of the sacrifices and dramas that had played out on that ancient ground. We were told about the cenote or water hole where they had found skeletons, and the ball game played with the head of some poor hapless person. The energies were very powerful and it was easy to feel the trauma of souls who had perished there. I hadn't realized the depth of the darkness that falls in the jungle, almost without warning. We made our way back to our bungalows, and I was feeling rather spooked but I told myself to not be so silly as I shut my door. I knew Alex was next door, but the feeling of all the spirits that seemed to be still stuck in trauma at their violent end seemed to have followed me back to my room. I tried to control my fear when I turned out the lights, lying on my bed listening to the cacophony of jungle sounds that erupted out of the night. It was so dark, I felt that there were so many presences in the room, including a guide that I had been introduced to back in England, a couple of years before, and who had made his presence felt when I was in America. I felt he was Quetzalcoatl and I could see him dancing around me with gold armbands and huge ingots in his earlobes and a feathered headdress. This would have been wonderful, if I hadn't been so scared. I tried to tell myself it was just my vivid imagination and to get a grip of myself. Right in the middle of this, there was a pounding on the door. I couldn't imagine who might be knocking on my door at that time of night. I had decided to keep my lights on as I was just too frightened to cope with the pitch black and creepy sounds. In trepidation I opened the door to find a terrified Karen apologizing for disturbing me, but she said she was so frightened and could she come and stay in my room. I burst out laughing and admitted to being just as petrified and that I was so glad to have some company, having got used to sharing a room with her over the past few days. We hugged each other and bolstered our courage by sharing the large double bed and dimmed lights that we didn't turn off for the rest of the night!

The next morning we had arranged to meet a guide to have a proper tour of the ruins. The pyramid was even more impressive in the daylight. As I quietly meditated about all the souls that had climbed its many steps and who had lived and worked in the complex, I began to feel the presence of the large whale shark, who had promised to re-connect with me, when

The Mayan ruins of Chichen Itsa

I arrived at the site. I was quite surprised that I could feel him so strongly and it was as though his beady eye was boring into me. He instructed me to create a huge light crystal orb etherically, above the pyramid, and then to imagine a beam of light shining up into the universe, connecting with the star system of Orion. I then visualized the light shining down into the great pyramid at Giza and then creating a triangle of light back from Egypt to Mexico, and the pyramid in front of me. I also felt like it was affecting all the pyramids on the planet. It has always fascinated me how the pyramid design has been replicated all over the world, since logically the ancient people would not have been able to compare notes on the construction of such a complex shape! I had no idea what this visualization would achieve; I just followed my guidance and prayed that it might bring some healing to the planet. It was obviously very important to Sonny that I complied with his wishes, and I once again marvelled at the wisdom of such a creature and the magnitude of the awareness that he must have for the planet.

We also visited the place where Quetzalcoatl lived and I found the energies there very moving as I felt so connected to him, especially as he had danced around my bed for most of the night. I thought that perhaps he and the whale shark were colluding, in order for me to listen to their guidance. I hoped I had served them well and that whatever healing or energetic reconnections were meant to occur, I had played some part in implementing it. The ruins were spectacular and we spent several hours exploring. There were many wonderful gifts for sale and I bought a large painted mask of the feathered serpent representing Quetzalcoatl, which I still have in my hallway at home. I feel it wards off negative energies, as it seems to be a very powerful artefact, holding some of the power of that ancient place.

Reluctantly, we left the ruins and our lovely hotel and journeyed back to Cancun where we were staying for a couple of nights before going home. We all felt bombarded with the frenetic energy of the city. After the island paradise and the incredible energies of the Mayan ruins, this touristy, nightclub hotspot felt horrible. I still felt the presence of Quetzalcoatl, but it felt dissipated by the heavy vibration of the city. We did however book a trip to Tulum, the site of the ancient Mayan port, as we had been told it was a beautiful site. We boarded the coach on an incredibly hot day. As we explored the site, I felt guided to place light crystals at various points around the site. I was amazed to read later in Drunvalo Melchizedek's work *The Serpent of Life beyond 2012*, that he had also visited Tulum and felt guided to place crystals there too.

Iguanas sunbathed on the ancient stone walls, and once again I imagined all the feet that would have trod the ancient paths around the complex as I placed mine, overlaying the prints of others who had passed before me. The sun was unbearable at midday, so we descended the well preserved wooden steps down to the beach. These steps would have been used for all the goods and provisions that would have sailed to this ancient site. We were all flagging in the heat so we walked into the waves fully clothed, holding our shoes above the water, relishing the coolness of the sea. As we were soon due to meet our coach, we reluctantly left the water and climbed back up the steps that led up the cliff face and again I pondered on all the ancient activity at that fabulous place.

The next year Jackie was running the trip again and I really felt that I could get more information from the wonderful sea beings. So I felt guided to go to Mexico once again, but this time to remain on the island to spend more time with the sharks, enjoying the special energy of the island. The weather was not so kind to us the second time, but the whale sharks were just as amazing. I also met a very patient cockroach. It had unusual black and white markings and was really quite beautiful. I had kept some wheat-free crackers in my room and was a little alarmed on opening the packet when the cockroach leapt out. I asked him if he might live on the covered decking for a few days if I put some food there for him. It was perhaps very unkind of me not to want to share my room – or his room, while I was there! He seemed okay with this and disappeared from sight under the door. I sat on the decking the next morning, staring out at the perfect vista just outside my room on the beach, when out of the corner of my eye I saw him waving his antennae, which seemed to signal that he wanted to tell me something. He looked a bit droopy and at first I thought he might have been injured as his legs seemed a little crumpled. However, as I sent him some healing, he suddenly seemed to stand right up on his legs and turn towards me. He said:

"Your work will become very well-known, it is imperative that you tell people about the messages from the animal kingdom, don't doubt your abilities, we wouldn't have asked you if you couldn't do the job!"

I told him how beautiful he was and he grew in stature even more as he seemed to dance around on the wooden railing. I apologized for asking him to leave, but he seemed to wave my words away with his antennae, and said that his species were much misunderstood and at least I hadn't tried to squash him! It reminded me that any creature large or small can have a profound message for us. I looked forward to the other messages I felt were about to come my way from the larger sea creatures I was about to meet once more. I wrote about the message I received from a common house fly about letting myself into my heart, instead of just thinking about everyone else, in my book *An Exchange of Love*, but I have since received two more messages from flies! I was running some courses in Portugal and I was relaxing by the pool after a tiring day teaching, when a fly landed on my arm and gave me the same purposeful expression of appearing to want to 'tell' me something. I sent out as much love as I could muster and the words I heard in in my head were *"You still don't know what you are truly capable of"*!

I was shocked and wondered what else I was capable of doing and when I would be shown these potentials. It all felt very exciting. Then last summer, I was having lunch outside in the sun and I was told by another fly that *"Things are hotting up"*! I questioned what that might mean and it felt as though my future purpose and life challenges were unfolding and manifesting much more quickly. The fly told me that I just needed to put the thought 'out there' and it would be created in my reality, which has proved to be the case!

Anyway, back to the island. I overheard a wonderful man called Eric talking about chakra systems in animals and I immediately introduced myself, as I thought this was a person I needed to talk to! (I had been working with the physical and higher soul chakras of animals, and I hadn't heard anyone else talking about their energy centres.) I was thrilled to find that he was a member of our group and that he and his daughter were to be on the boat with us over the next few days. We had some wonderful conversations about our encounters. We would both meditate and I would give him the information I had gleaned from the creatures and he would then expand on the information. This is the information he received from the whale sharks:

The place keepers

15-6-08

"We are the whale sharks. We have come because you asked us and are happy to do so. Please humour us because not many people speak to us and hear our story. It is simple yet profound. We are the place keepers. We provide the opportunity to those who wait. We are extremely patient beings that know no enemies. We have size and speed when we want it but we choose to linger in our movements because we are deep in our meditative trance of being. We dream in the stars, play with planets and eat to our heart's content. We are the place keepers because we help Mother Earth and every sentient being hold the space to create their dreams. We hold the intention to let things happen, just as people, beings and planets have dreamt them.

There is a pregnant moment where intention meets dream. Sometimes the energy it takes to create matter or action on earth is difficult or takes time. Our mission and intention is to help speed the process up, although it would be hard to imagine it looking at our slow pace, to help the universe manifest their dreams into matter. We hold the space and create energetics to help you hold your dream. We also create the space, the time and the opportunity to experience the fruits of your intentions by having your dreams come true.

To hold space is our joy. This is why you could not connect to us the way you have with other beings. We are always partly in the dreamtime holding the intention of love and happiness. Whale sharks hold the thread or cord with the Divine while connecting to your heart's desire, even the desire you are too afraid to speak. We sense these dreams as well and hold the space for you to manifest your heart's love, which you are too afraid to express. We hold the awareness, create the file of possibility to use computer terms and let you grow until your courage, events and opportunity, occur to let you move into your desire, love or place of dreamed contentment.

So when you are dreaming of a project, afraid to move forward in life, or paralyzed in fear or worry, come to us with your dreams. Let us swim into your life, mouth agape, dedicated and assured of the bounty of life to remind you to

swallow and enjoy life to your heart's content just as we do in the ocean. Our size lets you know that the world is bountiful and dreams become reality if you create the space for it. Come to us with your dreams and enjoy our dreamy eyes that see your heart's love through the veil. We will hold your deepest desires close to our heart until you have the courage to manifest them into your life.
Please hear our message. We are cousins of the whales, dolphins and mantas that you love. Work with all of us to make your dreams come true. We move towards our dreams when you swim with us. This lets you know that you need to move towards yours with love in your heart and dedicated intention. The world will nurture you and all you need to do is open your mouth, open your heart and walk into the bounty of the universe. We will meet you there with our bellies full and congratulate you when you get there."

—Love, peace and harmony, the whale sharks

These beautiful words completely resonated the feelings I got while in the water with these magnificent beings. We also spent time with the most fantastic giant manta ray. On our last trip, the mantas had seemed rather skittish and on the one occasion I had swum alongside of one, I had had trouble with my snorkel as the valve was letting in sea water. This time however, I had no such trouble and was blessed to be able to swim alongside and above the beautiful creature for as long as she wanted (for I felt it was a female).She had a wingspan of at least four metres and I felt very insignificant next to her. I mimicked her huge wings in silent flight, like a huge dark angel. She seemed to be purposefully swimming along the ocean floor, which was only about 30 feet beneath me. I asked her why she seemed to focus so intently on the ocean bed and she told me she was monitoring the oceanic grid lines. I was quite surprised at this, but watched her as she seemed to change course in a very methodical way. She wasn't feeding; she definitely seemed to be following some kind of invisible line. She told me that there were fractures in the grid lines and I asked her what had caused this. She said the most damaging thing to the lines were humans' negativity and fear. She also said she was balancing the energy for the new influxes that would come over the next few days of the equinox from the universe. At times she would rise to the surface and I swam right next to her enormous wings and unfurled mouth piece. Again gazing into this creature's wise eye was an amazing experience. I thanked her with all my heart for allowing me to be near her, and for her messages that were so profound. Eventually, I decided to check on where the other members of our group were and realized that I had been left in the water with her, as the others had returned to the boat. I couldn't see the boat, just a huge expanse of sea, so I did hope that they hadn't forgotten me and returned to the shore without me! Eventually the boat motored into sight, although I would have been happy to spend another couple of hours with the manta, I was rather tired after my long swim. I felt so lucky to have had the chance to spend time with her and I felt the universe had just created that window of time alone with her, where we could totally connect with each other. Back on the boat, I told Eric what she had told me, and he said he would ask for more clarity that night. This is what Eric received to expand on the grid line information:

Manta ray collective

"We come per your request and yes, indeed we do provide spiritual assistance to the planet, contrary to what many may think. We are angelic beings that provide stability to those around us. We provide safety to those that have none and eat only what we need. We love to help Gaia when we can. I was sending energy to correct energetic patterns that needed energetic support yesterday as Madeleine said. I loved being with you all and enjoyed your assistance for your joy helped me and Mother Earth. Your joy is the energy that powers the universe, and we live it every day. Thank you for your help and assistance. It was my pleasure to share the joy that is our experience every day. Cruising through the currents of the ocean, bathed in love and returning it back to dear Mother Earth that supports us was wonderful. She is going through a transformation and you are as well. We help with the

birthing pains but not really. We just help lubricate the evolution that is so necessary at this time of change. Thank you for your help for it was a joy for me as well as for you. This is the Divine energy of love at its finest."

I was blown away by the words that Eric channelled. He has a wonderful site on which he posts blogs of his communications and those of other people around the world. This information is in the resource section at the end of the book. I felt this was why I'd been guided to return to these fabulous waters and to connect with yet more wonderful sentient beings that we had so much to learn from, and their compassion for our treatment of Mother Earth. Once again, it was very hard to leave the island. On my last morning, I spent some time walking along the beach, gazing downwards at the myriad of shells that littered the shoreline in all their finery. I felt that I would love to bring just one tiny piece of paradise home with me, but struggled to choose just the right one. The words of this prose filled my head and I scribbled them down when I returned to my room.

The perfect shell

The sun beat down from the azure sky. Even in the early morning, its power made itself known to all that felt its rays. The soft surf gently lapped at my feet as I paddled in the frothy surge beneath me. Above me the frigate bird, wings outstretched, languidly floated on a thermal that caressed its flight. As the palms waved their salutations, I had to remind myself that this was no fantastical dream that I would be slow to relinquish to the dawn of a cold English morning. I was actually here, marvelling at the scene before me. This tropical wonder that stormed my senses with a sensory overload of joy pervaded my being. I began to observe the shells that crunched beneath my feet and tickled my toes in the shifting sand. I commenced searching aimlessly at first and then with more deliberation, for just the right souvenir to capture the splendour of the island and my brief sojourn in Paradise. I stooped to examine each one that caught my attention, only to discard it for a crack, or some lack of brilliance. This abalone was just a shard of pearlescent light. This little clam had a broken edge. This pattern was not quite uniform enough. Enough! Who was I to judge nature's perfect imperfections? Who was I to condemn with all my perceived frailties? Like the glorious island sunrise, it dawned on me that I was but a tiny shell on life's shoreline, to be loved for all my imperfections. Not judged or graded, but to be celebrated, cherished, and revered, as should every living organism on this planet if we but ditch our disdain, jettison our judgmentalism, curb our condemnations, free our spirit, and release our souls, accepting our magnificence, in the glory of creation.

I felt ashamed of my deliberations, but felt that at least I had got the message of what the shells were teaching me! They seemed to hold the energy of the sea like crystals, with their own special power. I drank in all the sights and sounds of my taxi journey to the airport, to capture my memories of that beautiful place. I was so glad that I had spent the whole time on the island, as I mingled with the throng of tourists looking rather worse for wear after their revelries. They had enjoyed themselves in a rather different way, but I was glad that I had been lucky enough to spend such blissful days with some of the world's most fascinating creatures.

The Egyptian dog and my return to Egypt

I had an email from Caroline, who I'd met on the whale trip in the Dominican Republic. She told me of an amazing experience with a group of people from Glastonbury that she had gone to Egypt with and that they were running another trip for the autumn equinox. She suggested I look at the proposed itinerary and see if I felt drawn to join them. It had been four years since my last visit to Egypt. There were two places that I had always felt drawn to visiting and I hadn't managed to get to either on my last trips, so when I read that we would be visiting Giza with the Sphinx and the pyramids and also Philae, I could hardly contain my excitement. We were to be anchoring in the divine feminine energy that was to be the new paradigm for the planet in 2012 and so, in order to balance that, we would visit the most masculine site of the Kings chamber in the great pyramid, and the most female site being the Isis temple at Philae.

This was the mission of the group intention that set my pulses racing:

We are asked to make a unique and essential contribution to all men and women everywhere on this beloved planet. To release the history of abuse between the sexes; to release the deep memories so we can affect the collective positively. This is the Healing of Souls. This is the time of great change. Be still and listen and let your heartbeat come into resonance with All That Is…

The group consisted of men and women who were to work together to help achieve this goal as an extension of Drunvalo Melchizedek's work in Egypt. We were given a list of books to read in preparation, including some of the 'Anastasia' books that I had not previously heard of. We also had a preparation weekend in Glastonbury in order to meet some of the group members who were to come from Sweden, Australia, Belgium, Iran,

Canada, England and Wales. They were a wonderful group and when we finally all met at Heathrow on the afternoon of our departure to Cairo, we all felt we 'knew' each other, and it was great to see Caroline again.

As the plane began its descent, I began to feel a familiar fluttering of excitement at the prospect of being on Egyptian soil once more. We were to stay in a hotel right in the energy field of the pyramids, as the town had encroached nearer and nearer to the iconic land marks, and so they were literally on our doorstep. Being able to look at the towering shapes on the horizon was breathtaking. However, we were due to fly to Aswan very early the next morning in order to visit Philae first. We managed to fit in a visit to the Cairo Museum, and I was eager to see the statues of Sekhmet and of course all the famous treasures that I had been fascinated by since childhood. The wealth of artefacts was almost too much to take in. As I searched for a sight of the lioness-headed goddess, I suddenly became aware of heat rushing through me, and as I rounded a corner I was met by a huge statue, whose leonine presence drew me in. I felt she was welcoming me home and thanking me for returning to my 'homeland'. She asked me to reconnect other members of the group, who were unaware of their lion-being heritage. One of the other women with me also felt a very strong connection. I was guided to place one hand on the statue and the other hand on my new friend, and she felt she was almost being branded as the heat seared into the palm of her hand. She joked that she expected to see a mark saying 'property of Sekhmet' when I took my hand away, as the heat had been so intense. I felt blessed to feel such a strong physical connection once again to the deity who I felt was my matriarch. Although I had felt her presence many times since our first reconnection in this lifetime at Karnak, it was still wonderful to return to Egypt, to feel the full strength of her power and to find others who had had lifetimes as lion beings or Paschats, as I discovered they were called. I had been enthralled reading the book *The Sirius Connection* by Murray Hope, as it triggered more memories, and here I was again meeting my past in my present incarnation.

We set our alarms very early next morning and arrived in time to catch the small plane that was to carry us along the Nile down to Aswan. Looking down on the magical river soon chased away our lethargy and I always felt that when I was near the life blood of Egypt I felt I'd come home. Aswan was truly beautiful and the hotel, being on the Nile, was sublime. We had some group meditations where we had been working to balance the planet and bring peace, symbolically calling in doves. After our group meeting, as I was wallowing in the cool water of the pool, a beautiful white dove landed on the step next to me, as though to affirm our wish to help bring healing to Mother Earth. It paddled about next to me for a few minutes and then flew off, leaving me in stunned wonder.

I loved the strange pachyderm-like rock formations of Elephantine Island and when we sailed above the waters that had consumed the original site of the temple at Philae, we all felt a huge sense of awe. We had fasted from the night before in preparation for our work. Alighting on the dock at the new home of the temple was very exciting and I trembled in anticipation as we connected with the beautiful energy of Isis. I felt she was also connected to Sirius, and with cetacean energies of the whales and dolphins. We had been guided to perform healing work on the nursery of lost children who had died and those souls who were waiting to incarnate. As we lay on the temple floor and prepared to visualize dropping beneath the subterraneous layers, a beautiful grey and white temple cat came and lay with us, as though guiding us on our journey. I visualized thousands of little orbs, twinkling at me. I felt they were the new souls waiting to be born. One in particular seemed to have the most beautiful energy and an almost 'Cheshire' cat-like smile. It told me that it was my granddaughter, who would be born to my eldest son and that she would be the catalyst for his spiritual re-awakening. Of all my children, he was the least open to spiritual matters and good-naturedly teased me about my endeavours. I thought it was interesting that this beautiful being had chosen to be his child. I couldn't wait to see the effect she was going to have on him! I also felt the presence of Lady Diana as a beautiful being in white. She seemed to be a guardian for the lost babies and I tried my hardest to send healing to all the beings there. As we came back from our healing journey, the cat, once she seemed content that we had all come back, stood up and with a flick of her tail, sauntered away. It was a very powerful and emotional experience and many group members were in tears. The cat had seemed to guide and protect us while we performed our tasks. I wondered how many other groups that cat had helped and what wonderful work it was still performing in its current role as a sacred feline.

This was our mission in connecting with the male energy of the great pyramid and the king's chamber.

Today is the autumn equinox!

*As the sun warms the stones of the Great Pyramid in the early
morning, we become aware of how many times we have visited this
great accumulator of energy in the past.
We are asked here to enter the tunnel with total respect and honour.
To be fully heart-centered, as it seems as if our heartbeat takes on the rhythm of
the pyramid, for this place is very much alive, and the stones breathe with the
magic of their creator. Your heart will quicken in anticipation as you find your
way to the entrance. You will ask the guardian's permission and when that is
received go forward into the darkness.
To bow your head and walk along the entrance tunnel of rough-hewn
rock, to the steep incline, leading to the Grand Gallery of a Thousand Steps,
every step echoing as if through aeons of time. We begin to sing the ancient chant
of the initiates, which echoes and resounds through all the spaces of the Great
Pyramid. Every breath becoming conscious. Your soul's purpose draws you
onward and upward with your hands pulling on the cold metal rails, your feet
seeking the next foothold. The sound of your breathing seems to fill the space.
The vastness wraps around you and the soft air murmurs. The feeling of
closeness of friends from many lifetimes comforts you. And the
feeling that others as yet unseen are waiting to welcome you. Waiting*

to be with you. *Bowing your head again almost bent double now you push*

forward through the Antechamber and into the Kings Chamber.

You breathe deeply. You are home. At last you can remove your shoes and find

your place. All the brothers and sisters gather now in reverence,

in the unfathomable depths of the silence. The tiny speck of light from

a single candle in the centre glows brighter. The first om begins...

Our intention today is to heal all that is not of love, all misqualified energies

and all pain and suffering that has existed between men and women since the

beginning of our time. Each one of us will stand as a pillar of a temple, complete

and whole. Each one of us carries a lineage that will be present through time and

space, but above all, it will be the deep desire from the depths of our hearts to offer

forgiveness from levels we have yet to explore. To offer solace and comfort and to

set a paradigm in the collective consciousness where all atrocities can be erased.

This day, the universe will take a deep breath, as we take a deep breath,

to begin again. We will be calling all the shamans through time and space,

all of the Inner Earth Cities, all the Great Cosmic Beings, the Ascended Masters

and all the Angels and Archangels to be our witness here.

We will do this with the utmost love and the knowing that the vision for the

New Earth is of happy families, who can grow together in understanding and

harmony to build the New World. And that the children who are coming forth,

these precious children in full consciousness, will be received and known for who

they are. This is our heart's desire. May it always be so.

Later, we will pay our respects to the Great Goddess Tefnut, who is the Sphinx.

Tefnut, with the body of a lion and a head that has been altered to that of a

Pharaoh, can be seen on the inner levels as the beautiful goddess she truly is.

Her inscrutable gaze looks towards the dawn and beyond into the cosmos to her

partner many light years away. The Star Gate was opened in March of this year

and links the two great lion beings across time and space. The significance will not

be lost upon you. Perhaps as we sit quietly in the sunlight, your past initiations in

these places of great power will merge into one. Allow your deep memory to bring

them into your heart. This great initiation of the human soul where finally peace

and deep love can abide. We will be meditating above the Divine Doorway where

the Destiny Stone sits between the Paws of the Sphinx, allowing our consciousness
to drop deep into the Earth connecting with the initiation tunnels and the Inner
City beneath the Giza Plateau, dedicated to Osiris.

Although feeling the energy of Isis was wonderful, I couldn't wait to feel the power of the great pyramid during our private time and to stand in front of the giant Sphinx at last on our return to Giza. We flew back to Cairo full of anticipation and booked into a hotel that had been a former palace, still opulent with its ornate decor. You could look out of a bedroom window and be dwarfed by the great pyramid barely a few hundred yards away. A few of us were definitely feeling the energies and were clearing much of the past. Unfortunately, a side effect of this was the frequent need to visit the toilets, which was a little worrying as the conveniences were not always convenient! I didn't feel it was the food I had eaten as we had all eaten different things, but several of us were similarly affected! However I prayed that I would not succumb while inside the King's chamber. Fortunately, we all managed to concentrate on the matter in hand. We had rehearsed our group formation and chants for when we would be working in the chamber. We also chose to sing John Lennon's *Imagine,* as we felt the words were most appropriate for world peace. We arrived by coach at the Giza plateau very early in the morning. I knew that the great pyramid was going to be big, but I wasn't prepared for the sheer scale and perfect construction of this wonder of the world. Climbing up the stone blocks to the entrance was a feeling I shall never forget. Because it was so early, the lights had not been put on, so we made the climb through the pyramid in almost complete darkness. In front of me was the large stocky form of Bennie, a Swede, and I was grateful for his sturdy body and beautiful deep voice chanting in front of me as I struggled to put any claustrophobic fears out of my head. Being so cramped and dark, we stooped and stumbled up the low-ceilinged pathways. I allowed myself to be carried by the chant further and further into the bowels of the pyramid, and with my hand on Bennie's shoulder we climbed up the final steps into the great chamber.

One of our group lit a small candle and I saw my first glimpse of the famous sarcophagus. I was amazed at the precision of the rocks that had been constructed into perfectly smooth walls. The acoustics were incredible. We took our positions in our rectangular formation, with chosen members being the corner stones to hold the energy of the group. We called in the deities and all beings that wished to work with us and the energy within the chamber became electric. Poor Caroline dropped like a stone and hit the hard floor with a sickening thud. Another Canadian girl also left her body and fell as we connected to the crystalline structures of the planet. I shuddered and swayed, holding Bennie's hand, and then knelt to place my white shawl under Caroline's head. She gradually came back into her physical body and cautiously sat up. Apart from a few bruises, she was absolutely fine. While we were connecting to the crystals, I felt that my whole skeleton had become crystalline and that I was glowing inside. When we sang *Imagine*, it was incredibly moving and the resonance of the acoustics was wonderful. I don't know what John would have thought about our rendition, but we did our best! We took turns lying in the sarcophagus which felt like an interstellar portal. I had a massive reconnection with one of the group members who I realized had travelled from Sirius with me. As we descended the steps the chanting reverberated around the chamber and the inner pathways. I felt that we had accomplished our task in helping to anchor in the feminine energy of the planet after thousands of years. I felt other planetary energies that seemed to celebrate as we made our way back to the entrance, in jubilant mood. It had been a privilege to spend private time and to be part of an incredible group; however, we seemed to have gained a new member. Climbing down the huge stone blocks at the front of the pyramid we were joined by a sandy coloured dog with beautiful soft brown eyes. She seemed to be congratulating us and we made a great fuss of her. Then suddenly, without us noticing, she vanished.

As if this wasn't enough, we were then taken to the Sphinx, and just standing in the sheer power of its presence was almost overwhelming. It felt like I'd waited all my life to be standing in that spot. My heart began

We were greeted and congratulated by a beautiful dog

to pound, as I felt that I was connecting with its heart. I could feel its heartbeat pulsating out of its mighty chest. The whole structure seemed to take on the living form of a lion, and as I trembled in front of its giant paws I felt we became as one, reconnecting with my leonine heritage. I cried at the thought of having to leave after waiting so long to connect to the famous being that seemed to have been waiting patiently for eons for people to understand its meaning. I was lucky enough to be given a meditation to connect with the Sphinx whenever I want to, surprisingly by my rescue dog Winnie, which you too can work with in the final chapter. I was sad at having to leave after such a short pilgrimage, but I was allowed a bonus experience of a visit to a family living in the Sphinx village, in the path of the of the energy line emitting from the huge lion.

We were hoping to meet a keeper of the ancient Khemit wisdom, ancient Egyptian knowledge, called Abd'el Hakim, but sadly he had died just before we arrived. Our leader had met him on many occasions, and their discussions had been wonderfully enlightening about sacred sites and their importance and relevance to planetary healing and our current task.

As we sat on the veranda sipping mint tea, I gazed down the street looking directly at the Sphinx, which still sent shivers through my body and I had difficulty not to shape-shift into my lion form, which seemed to be happening more and more! I could feel the presence of Hakim all around us and I felt he was laughing. We were told that he had a wonderful sense of humour and we all felt his joy at our visit. His daughter was to hold the wisdom for the future and we were so grateful to the grieving family for allowing us to pay our respects. Hakim's son carved the most wonderful statuettes and figures from the local limestone, out of which the pyramids were hewn. I had noticed some beautiful leonine/Sekhmet-like pieces and one in particular seemed to be 'bleeping' at me. The craftsman told me the price as I admired his work, but the statue was very expensive, so I had to say that I couldn't afford it. He seemed totally unperturbed by this and we just had the most wonderful 'liony' connection of bizarrely rubbing cheeks, as lions do when they greet each other. The other group members wondered what we were doing as it seemed quite an intimate exchange between two complete strangers. We just knew we 'knew' each other from many lifetimes ago as lion beings. Little did I know that Bennie had been listening to our dialogue and had secretly paid for the statue and bought it for me as a thank you present for some past life trauma healing I had performed for him. He had been in a lot of physical discomfort and since my healing he had been pain free. He had to return later on that day to collect it so that I would be unaware and totally surprised when it was presented to me. I was so thrilled.

We returned to our hotel for lunch and some of us decided that we would like to visit the other pyramids, one of which was open to the public. One group member, from Iran, felt that he had a massive connection with the pyramid, and every time he visited Egypt he felt drawn to lie in the sarcophagus, as though it was built for him. We decided to have a camel ride around the Giza plateau first, and I was given a beautiful camel called Abdul. He had the most wonderful patterns shaved into his fur down his neck and brightly coloured tassels and saddle. It was wonderful riding out with the other camels and our guide rode the most fabulous Arab horse. As we rode through the narrow streets towards the sandy plateau, we saw beautiful stallions being trotted out, showing off their elegant paces. I loved the gentle swaying of the camel's motion and it felt strangely familiar, as though it was yet another facet of a past life. It was beautiful surveying the magical vista of the plateau. I thanked Abdul for carrying me on our journey around the ancient grounds. He seemed quite content with his lot and was obviously well cared for by his owner.

We then decided to walk out onto the plateau to visit the smaller pyramids. It was mid afternoon and incredibly hot. Striding through the sand was quite tiring as the sun beat down on us. But the heat outside was nothing to what we encountered when going down into the pyramid of Khafre, still showing some of the ancient white covering that the pyramid would have had when it was constructed. We saw tourists coming out drenched in sweat and we soon realized why as we started to climb down the steps into the sauna-like conditions below. My Iranian friend lay in 'his' sarcophagus and then asked if we would like to see what it felt like. The guards fortunately didn't seem to mind, so I determined to try the experience. As I lay on the cold stone surface, I felt my heart begin to beat and then palpitate until I was sure it was about to explode. I was aware of streams of light pouring into my heart from other beings that felt like a mix of outer planetary energies. I had previously meditated and felt I had conversed with members of a galactic council and I felt similar energies now. I felt they were sensing my energy and observing the changes within me and the work we had endeavoured to accomplish on our mission, working with the earth's kundalini and the divine feminine energy. I asked if they could be a little gentler, as I wasn't quite sure how much more my heart could take, and I felt the energy gently recede. It was an incredible experience and I felt very blessed to have had such a powerful exchange with the beautiful beings. They seemed very concerned with the health of our planet and I was told that they were helping us help the earth, as what affected the earth affected their planets also. It is an experience that

I will never forget and I committed myself to continue helping the planet in whatever way I was guided.

As we climbed up out of the pyramid, we also had the drenched look of the other tourists exiting the heat of the interior. It was almost cool outside as there was a gentle breeze, which dried our damp skin. We staggered back to the hotel with our minds buzzing from our personal experiences and somehow found the energy to walk back through the sand. We all fell into our respective showers and then met for a final de-briefing of the day's events and messages that so many of us had received. We were all sad to have to leave at the end of a wonderful journey with lots of memories to last a lifetime. We all hoped to return to the land of the Pharaohs again one day to continue our work in whatever way was most appropriate.

India, the Andaman Islands and the elephants

"Pain shouts a reason — listen to reason."
—Wisdom from the elephant consciousness

"How would you like to swim with an elephant in the Indian Ocean?"my friend Jackie asked me. I had made several journeys with her to wonderful locations before and the prospect of being able to visit the most beautiful islands and meet a very special elephant was just too good an opportunity to miss! There were quite a few of us that had been lucky enough to participate in Jackie's 'wild ocean adventures' and she was always planning to create new experiences for us and researched avidly for the best, most respectful, crews and boats. She only chose companies that were non-invasive to wild creatures and worked to conserve wildlife and marine creatures. So when she found out about the old logging elephant that roamed Havelock Island, in the Andaman Islands, which had newly been opened to divers, she was keen to take us there. I said yes immediately and raided my adventure fund for the deposit. I wanted to experience the energy of the ocean and hopefully connect with the sea creatures and intuit planetary information from the elephants.

We would have to fly from Chennai in India to get to the islands, so we felt we should explore some of the mainland before our week there. I booked my flight to Delhi so that we could meet up and then travel to Jaipur and then on to Agra to see the iconic Taj Mahal, which had been on my wish list of things to do. It felt touristy rather than spiritual, but I really wanted to feel the energy there, as it was a symbol and demonstration of love for the Maharaja's departed wife. At one stage, the costs of the trip seemed to be spiralling and I wondered if I could justify spending the money on what seemed to be a bit of a 'jolly'. However, when I tuned into the elephants, I was told that the Andaman elephant had messages for me, and that I had to go and connect with this special being. So of course my doubts disappeared and I knew that meeting him was going to be very important.

Even so, I did wonder what I was doing and whether I should just try and find the next flight home when I arrived at Delhi airport. I waited alone for almost two hours, receiving some alarming glances from the men, a couple of which came up to me and asked if I wanted to go with them to a hotel. I waited outside the airport, but seemed to attract even more unwanted attention, so went back inside the arrivals lounge, wondering what I was going to do next. I contemplated trying to find a hotel and hoped that Jackie would ring back in reply to my increasingly worried messages! There was suddenly a commotion at one of the entrances and I turned to see Jackie pleading with a rather officious guard to be let in to look for me. I was so relieved to see her and practically ran to the guard saying it was okay – I was coming out! She apologized and explained that their taxi driver had waylaid them to go and look at carpets! I was to discover that the drivers were a law unto themselves and we had to let go of our need to get anywhere on time. There seemed to be a definite 'India time'. Anyway, I scrambled into the back of the taxi and we set off for Jaipur.

I drank in all the sights and sounds of a country I had only ever seen on television documentaries. I was amazed at the cattle strolling around the maelstrom of traffic that cascaded around roundabouts and frenetic streets. Constant honking of horns seemed to be the order of the day, and the three wheeler taxis diced with death as they weaved in between lorries and buses. It was fascinating witnessing the mêlée, but not so much fun when we were part of the manic rush to get through the streets and we were later to experience the full extent of the challenge of driving in India.

We arrived at our hotel in Jaipur which was beautiful, with ornate carvings and furnishings and I loved the whole energy of the city with its impressive city walls and palaces. The next morning we went to visit the city palace and had an elephant ride up to the palace. Our elephant was called Bubbly and she was beautifully decorated. I felt really guilty being carried by her up the steep path in the heat as we swayed to her gentle gait. I asked her how she felt about her work, which was day in, day out, carrying tourists up the hill to the palace. She said she had chosen her role, as she was teaching us about patience and acceptance. I felt very sad for her and tried to give her some healing when we had climbed off her lofty back. We had a very special moment of connection, where I felt the enormity of her being and rather like the dolphins in captivity, I felt she had chosen to be an ambassador of her species, who could teach us so much and affect so many people perhaps without them realizing. I felt very humble and honoured to have met her and again was astounded at the level of compassion a creature can have for man, who mainly saw them as a money-making commodity. This gentle giant then turned and lumbered back down the hill to collect her next load of tourists to be transported up to the palace. I was to learn far more about the 'elephant consciousness' later, when I met Rajan the Andaman elephant.

The gentle beauty of Jaipur faded as we left to travel to Agra for the sunset over the Taj Mahal. I was sitting in the front seat of the taxi and Jackie and three American guys were in the back. I'd met two of them before on our trips, and they were great fun, but even they were beginning to become uncomfortable with the erratic judgement of our driver and the other vehicles on the crowded roads. There was a feeling of inevitability as we were suddenly hit by another car trying to overtake us and then ran out of room as another car was in front of them. We were sent into a terrifying spin and braced ourselves for the car to flip over as we span round in front of the traffic. We smashed into the central reservation, sending our luggage flying into the oncoming traffic. Thank goodness there was a barrier, as we would certainly have been killed by the thundering traffic bearing down on us from the other oncoming lanes. We were all shaken but fortunately none of us were hurt. The taxi was rather worse for wear and the driver seemed very agitated. The guys in our group managed to grab our luggage and we huddled on the side of the road amidst a crowd that had gathered to discuss our experience. When we walked back down the side of the road to examine the extent of our skid marks, we were amazed to see a small roadside statue of Ganesh, the elephant-headed god. I hoped that it had been his influence that had saved us from injury or a worse fate. I thanked him fervently for his protection and maybe Rajan knew that I was on my way to meet him, to hear what he had to say and just maybe I could spread his message. I liked to think that the elephant had saved us in some way.

We waited for hours for another taxi to come, our luggage in tatters and the light fading. All thought of seeing the Taj Mahal at sunset faded as it got dark. We were warned that it was unwise to be sitting on the roadside with our possessions, but there was nothing we could do as we were in the hands of the taxi company. Our driver tried to repair the broken axle and the roof rack. We really thought the vehicle was a write-off, but even with a very wobbly rear wheel he decided it could be driven. None of us wanted to travel in it, but when the replacement taxi arrived there was not enough room for all of us and our luggage, so one of the guys bravely opted to travel in the limping taxi, with the luggage crammed into the back and the rest of us piled into the other car. It was completely dark by now, and even more frightening, as we frequently rushed up behind a cart being pulled by a camel, encountered vehicles with no lights and drivers on the wrong side of the road. I shut my eyes and prayed to Ganesh and any other gods who might hear our pleas, wrapping us in light.

We screeched into the hotel forecourt and shakily stepped out of the car, all of us relieved that our journey had ended without further mishap! We heard that another American had not been so lucky as she had been knocked off her scooter and killed by a bus on that very road.

We managed to find our rooms and as we were exhausted by the day's events, we collapsed into our beds, looking forward to at least witnessing the glory of the Taj Mahal early next morning. Our taxi arrived to take us to the palace and we queued to enter the beautiful grounds. Stepping through the archway and viewing the famous structure beautifully reflected in the water in front of us was a stunning image. Watching the light change as the sun moved across the sky was incredible and once again, I had to pinch myself to make sure I was actually there! The semi-precious stones inlaid in the white marble inside were so beautiful and we marvelled at the commitment to build such a wonderful token of love.

We then had the prospect of being taxied back to Chennai where we were to catch our flight to the Andamans. We asked the driver to take his time as we didn't want a repetition of the day before. However, we found it was still better to close your eyes and pray! Our check-in time came and went and we were all getting quite edgy as there weren't any other flights that day. The driver seemed quite unperturbed as he doubled back on himself, seemingly not knowing quite where he was! Eventually, we saw the airport signs and he pulled up in front of departures. We frantically threw money at him, grabbing our luggage as quickly as we could from the vehicle and raced to the check-in. The process seemed excruciatingly slow and we knew that we were seconds away from missing our flight. We leapt onto the already loaded airport bus, moments before the doors closed and made the flight by the skin of our teeth. We were all shaking with relief and the stress of the journey and I've never been so glad to take my seat on a plane in all of my life.

The Andamans

We had to queue for visas as the Andamans are a restricted area and we were all eager to get to the ferry that would take us to our island and our small barefoot eco resort. None of us had visited the islands before and we were thirsty to drink in the scenery. At the dock of Havelock Island, there were some jeeps waiting to collect us. There were some unusual goats frolicking about the area, with rather alien-like eyes, and it felt like they were greeting us. We raced along the narrow tracks, again experiencing the Indian way of driving as we played chicken with a large bus coming straight towards us. I closed my eyes, calling on all my protective guides, who of course didn't fail me and we bumped on down the tracks past fields with water buffalo grazing or working with their human counterparts. It was a fascinating place with very meagre abodes for the families living there. The thatched buildings were breathtaking and we could hear the sound of the surf as the ocean crashed on to the shore. We were shown to our jungle huts which were amazing, with intricately woven ceilings that created the thatched roofs. The tropical birds serenaded us from the the treetops as the sun began to set. I decided to find the beach so I could watch the sunset over the ocean. As I ventured down the path indicated by the sign, I was drawn to a large tree on the periphery of the shoreline. There were a few scattered branches, but nothing to indicate why the tree felt so important, but I was to discover the next day when we met Rajan how significant the tree was. I was also unprepared for the sight that met my eyes as I stepped out onto the beach that was rather unflatteringly called 'Beach Number Seven'. It was glorious, and the reflections of the pink and purple hues mirrored in the water were spectacular. I waited until the sun fell into the ocean horizon, and then started to make my way back through the paths, saluting the tree as I passed.

We had a wonderful meal in the thatched restaurant and overheard tales of the fantastic diving on the reefs and the sea life that abounded in the pristine waters. However, although we were excited about exploring the reefs, we were all waiting with anticipation at the prospect of meeting our pachyderm friend the next morning. A final trip to the beach to sit and wonder at the myriad of stars in the unpolluted sky led me to give thanks to the universe for blessing me with the wonderful experiences, and the beauty of Mother Earth that she was sharing with me. The frogs chorused my walk back to my hut, and I fell into my mosquito netted four poster bed and dreamt about my beautiful dog Nessie. She had been a wolfhound/deerhound cross, and was an gentle giant of a dog. It had broken my heart to have to re-home her when my marriage broke up. I had found her a marvellous new home and had kept telling her that it was because I loved her so much, that she deserved the very best home and that I was unable to give that to her anymore. She had settled in well and had visited me in my dreams previously which had given me a mixture of sweet and sad emotions. However, I had been devastated to hear that she had to be put to sleep because of bone cancer and I greatly mourned her loss. But here she was right in my face; my dream so real, that I could feel her soft grey brindle coat and vividly felt the soft gaze of her beautiful brown eyes that melted your heart, under her bushy expressive eyebrows. I could feel her leaning against me as if to say "I'm fine, I'm with you, don't be sad". I awoke with tears pouring down my face with the joy of feeling her presence so clearly. I felt she was healed in spirit, and that she had come to reassure me. The jungle sounds at night reminded me of my time at Chitzen Itza, but no ghostly presences jarred my nerves. I just sank back into bed, and dreamed about our imminent meeting with the awesome elephant.

I awoke early as the dawn chorus deafened me through the thin walls of the hut. The sun was rising and I could make out the distant surf that caressed my senses. I hurriedly dressed and joined the others for our first encounter with Rajan. He was to be found breakfasting on coconuts and branches. He was a huge ancient beast with impressive tusks and his wonderful dexterous trunk effortlessly tossed the nuts into his mouth as he crunched down on the shells. The magnitude of his presence is hard to describe. His sad eyes held so much wisdom, and I thanked him from the bottom of my heart for allowing us to meet with him and asked him if he felt like swimming that day, would he mind us joining him? His Mahout Nazru didn't speak English but we gesticulated our thanks with hand gestures, and gave him some money for his family. Rajan 'told' me of his sadness at the loss of his elephant wife who had been bitten by a snake and had died. This turned out to be true and he also showed me metal hooks that were used as tools by the loggers to force him to work. Luckily, he was now allowed to roam the island with his kind friend Nazru who looked after his needs. There were also two female elephants on the island that he could meet with, but I felt they could never replace his departed matriarch.

After , we were to meet up at the beach around ten o'clock to see if Rajan wanted to swim. We got into our swimming and snorkelling gear, the divers preparing their cameras and tanks. We had some wonderful underwater photographers with us from America and Japan, who were eager to get the shots of the elephant above them in the sea. We made our way into the turquoise water and hoped that Rajan would oblige us with his morning dip. The exercise was very good for his ancient joints, and the sea water medicated an old sore on his shoulder. After a few moments, Rajan lumbered down the sandy beach and entered the warm water. We had been instructed about the elephant etiquette and maintained our positions. I thanked him again for allowing us to swim with him and invade his hydrotherapy! He patiently allowed us to free dive and photograph him from beneath, and kindly tolerated the flashing cameras. You had to be a little careful when he changed direction, as his huge tusked head would turn and his pounding legs would paddle through the water at an alarming angle if you happened to be right next to him. Seeing the sheer tonnage of the beast floating above you was an awesome sight. Seeing his belly and the soles of his flat toe-nailed feet from underneath was an incredible privilege. The water was so clear, until on one occasion I had been trying to practise my free-diving skills, and the water had seemed to get a little murky. I bobbed to the surface only to narrowly miss sporting a new headdress of elephant poo! It would have been most unpleasant inhaling that particular gift from Rajan down my snorkel! But it was wonderful being in the sea with him as he generously shared his time with us. I kept thanking him and asked him if he could impart any information that I needed to know whenever he felt able and more importantly, when I was ready to hear it.

There were many wonderful snorkelling and diving experiences. The tropical fish were amazing. Our American underwater photographer said "It looks like God ate a whole bunch of Crayola and threw up all over down there!" His meaning was that the diversity of the colours and combinations of colours and patterns of the sea creatures were beyond any human imaginings. I fell in love with beautiful fish called Oriental Sweet Lips, Moorish Idols, Tangs and many others. Their beauty transfixed me as I gazed down through my mask in the crystal-clear water. There was a beautiful blue lagoon just a few hundred yards along the beach. You could wade out into the shallow water and then just look down and swim a little way from the shore and beneath you was breathtaking beauty as the small schools of gorgeous fish darted around the rocks. I swam over the craggy home of a very large, huge girthed, purple moray eel, who glowered at me with his glumly expressive tooth-lined mouth. I apologized for disturbing him and was quite happy to swim away leaving him in peace! I was concentrating on a beautiful school of fabulous small orange coloured fish whose fluorescence shimmered in the light, when a huge grouper seemed to appear right next to me out of nowhere. It really made me jump and his rather sour expression made it clear that he was unimpressed with me invading his ocean. I apologized again which seemed to slightly appease him. I told him how wonderful he was, and how lucky I was to meet him, but I'm not sure he was convinced! Everyone laughed when I told them that I had been spooked by a grouper, having swum with lots of enormous creatures in the past. It was just that I wasn't expecting something so large and fierce looking suddenly being that close. I thought there would only be small fish in those shallow waters. I almost bumped into another moray – this time green, not as large as the first but commanding respect nonetheless, so I left him to his watery world and swam on.

We took the boat out to some much deeper waters for the other party members to dive. My snorkel buddy Bill and I enjoyed snorkelling around, relishing the sights except for one area that seemed to be swarming with jelly fish, so we stayed onboard and left the dancing jellies to their ocean choreography. On one occasion, I was clambering over the edge of the boat with my fins on and I had a warning voice in my head, asking me to be careful. I told myself I was being careful, but nevertheless managed to slip as I attempted to place my feet on the rung of the metal ladder, on the side of the boat. I slammed into the metal as one leg rammed down behind the ladder. If I hadn't been able to sit in the water I would have broken my leg. I sported some fabulous bruises for several weeks. We had a lot of fun though and we watched out for each other as we snorkelled around the reefs. It was a wonderful opportunity for all of us to experience the fantastic reefs that had been closed to divers for so long, and I sent lots of love to all the sea creatures and hoped they would be safe with the influx of human attention. I thanked them for allowing us to invade their space and hoped we hadn't disturbed them too much.

We were invited to share Rajan's afternoon bath in the freshwater pool that he liked to bathe in to wash the salt water out of his gnarled skin. We followed him along the jungle track and he stopped at a beach cafe where there was a hose pipe. Nazru turned on the tap and Rajan held the pipe with his trunk and poured the jet of water into his mouth. He would then tip his huge head backwards and take a huge gulp and then repeat the process. He must have drunk gallons of water and then he sprayed himself and us with water for good measure! He lumbered into the pool and then Nazru cajoled him into lying down for a scrub. His head was almost submerged but the tip of his trunk peeped out of the surface of the water, so that he could still breathe. His gargantuan body then contorted so that he could flop the other side of his vast body into the cool fresh water. He seemed to love the process and his ancient limbs creaked at the effort of his daily ablutions, in idyllic surroundings.

The small resort offered massage facilities, so I thought I would treat myself. The massage room was up a hill so I embarked on what I thought would be a gentle five minute stroll and ended up staggering up a long steep incline that seemed to never end, and eventually stumbled into the

My special moment of connection with Bubbly

therapy hut. I wasn't prepared for the treatment I received from a rather handsome but slightly bored young man. Perhaps if I'd been 20 years younger he might have been a little more interested. There were no gentle discreet towels to shelter my modesty. I was told to take everything off except my briefs and lie face up on the couch. There were also no screens so anyone could have just waltzed in and been met with a rather scary sight! I was well and truly massaged in parts I didn't know I had. I rather liked it initially as the warm oil was dripped over my body, but this young man obviously was intent on leaving no area unpummelled. I kept thinking to myself – was it supposed to be like this? I found it hard to relax, as I was exposed to all and sundry, but did my best to surrender to the thorough hands of my therapist. No place for my bashful, British reserve here! The rest of the party thought it was hilarious when I emerged from the jungle and told them what had transpired. They didn't seem convinced that it would have been normal practise, but I put it down to experience and the group seemed to enjoy the antics of their oldest member as I regaled them with my tales from the therapy couch!

Early on our last morning, I finally realized the significance of the tree that had seem to draw me when I first ventured into the jungle. It was another of Rajan's favourite dining spots, which explained the scattering of branches on the jungle floor. I saw him tucking into his favourite branches and understood why it was such a special spot. The following are some notes that I jotted down whilst leaning against 'his' tree, when he was away visiting other parts of the island. It felt like I was more able to quieten my mind and 'listen' to his messages, rather like the whales had shown me in my bunk. It's hard to not get overwhelmed by the enormity of the experience, when you're up close and personal. My experiences have been so incredible – that it's difficult to still your mind when all you want to say and feel is "oh wow, oh wow"! Leaning against his tree gave me the perfect opportunity to tune in and hear what he had to say.

"Willingness to serve in order to teach. He carries the profound pain of the elephant consciousness. When I tap into that, even for a minute, it becomes overwhelming and intolerable. He teaches me about pain and its uses. "Pain shouts a reason – listen to reason" pre-quoted even before I met him. He carries the pain of the other elephants, even from the time of Hannibal – those that perished in the cold Himalaya with Hannibal. They went so far, but so many perished. Sitting beneath Rajan's tree, where the remnants of his 'snacks' lay strewn on the jungle floor, I see huge branches that he tosses into his mouth with his wonderful trunk. I sit here to feel his vibrations and energy and visualize his beautiful sad eyes that have witnessed so much. He tells me that he has had many incarnations, both as elephant and Mahout, in order to experience both sides of the coin. His higher chakra systems connect to the star systems Orion and Veda. He has constellations surrounding him and is a true star being. He is so generous with us as he patiently lumbers into the water so we can get our 'shots'. Nazru cajoles and taps him with a wooden stick – not the metal hooks that Rajan showed me being used by the loggers. He showed me visually and emotionally, the

pain of female elephants being separated from their young, in order to work with
the loggers, but they had to take up their role of servants as Bubbly had done in
Jaipur to teach us those lessons of acceptance and patience. As the crabs creak
through the jungle litter, I marvel at the role these wonderful creatures undertake
in order to carry our pain. "The flagship species is doing a wonderful job." The
sound of the surf echoes behind me, and the jungle birds chatter. Rajan's not at
his usual spot for breakfast so I hope he's enjoying a jungle repast somewhere
before he gives us our last ocean encounter. I question whether it is my role to help
to heal his pain. I'm told that I must not interfere. I wrap him in light and hope
that it will help him 'endure' his pain for this lifetime and help him help us. Does
he need a soul retrieval? (This is a technique the horses had taught me to release
past life trauma) I'm told that he has to carry that pain in order to fulfil his role
in this incarnation. What an immense being and hugely evolved soul, which
would be willing to carry this for the planet."

I had watched a documentary before I left for my trip to India, about
the gathering of around 3,000 elephants at a specific location in Africa.
There didn't seem to be any logical reason for the choice of location as it
wasn't a significant watering hole, but it seemed that all these elephants
seemed driven to gather there. They were filmed interacting and folding
their trunks around each other as though imparting information to one
another. It was an amazing film and concluded that maybe there were
ley lines or energy centres that called them there to connect with each
other and that they were exchanging knowledge. It certainly seemed like
they were on a mission to reconnect with each other, and I realized that
this must be the elephant consciousness that Rajan was showing me. The
very last words spoken by the narrator were "the flagship species of the
planet is doing a great job"! I reflected that indeed they were, and that if
these fantastic creatures could be allowed to survive and flourish, then it
would be a good indication that just maybe we could allow the rest of the
planet to flourish as well. Yet more evidence of the necessity for mankind
to listen to the wisdom of animals.

We returned to the frenetic energy of Chennai in a much more relaxed fashion without any nerve-wrenching dashes to the airport. We had gazed longingly back at the island as we floated away on our little ferry. I had made a final pilgrimage to the fabulous Beach No. Seven and sent out a wave of love from my heart, thanking the universe for blessing me with all the experiences I had been privileged enough to have. Rajan was off somewhere around the island and I sent him our love and thanks for all his wisdom. Landing back at Chennai was a real culture shock in contrast to the gentle energy of the island. I longed for the sound of the surf, and the jungle sounds lulling me to sleep, instead of the constant honking cacophony of traffic that incessantly roared past our hotel. On my last night on the island, it wasn't so peaceful, as I thought there was a pack of werewolves outside my flimsy walled hut! I had just drifted off to sleep when I began to hear some very eerie growling and shuffling sounds on the veranda just next to my room, sounding as though whatever it was could break down the rush wall of my hut with one swipe. My imagination ran riot as I lay there not daring to look out and see what was going on. There would suddenly be high-pitched screaming and then horrific scuffles and fighting of what sounded like several beasts. I implored them to be gentle with each other and to leave each other alone – if only so I could get some sleep, but I did want whatever they were to be unscathed. When morning came and the sound seemed to have abated, I ventured gingerly out of my door, to find blood all over the veranda. Apparently, there was a pack of wild unneutered dogs roaming the island and they seemed to have chosen my veranda on which to have a mighty battle over a bitch in season, as she lay on my doorstep. I saw five or six dogs being chased away by the resort groundsman. I felt rather silly after my wild imaginings in the inky darkness of the night, but they had thrashed against the thin walls of my hut and I really felt they would be joining me at any minute! I still preferred the fracas of the wild dogs to the man-made din of Chennai.

I had some very interesting dreams and visualizations whilst trying to zone out of the noise. As I was trying to drift off, I decided to go through a chakra meditation, where you can check in on each chakra and invite a picture or a colour to indicate energetically what is going on in each energy centre. All my lower chakras had positive images or clear colours but as I reached my throat chakra, I was met with an illuminating image of a gasping fish in a goldfish bowl, which was obviously lacking oxygen. I thought this was rather interesting as the throat chakra is the seat of our self-expression, so I wondered what I was not able to express? I visualized white light pouring into the image and it evolved into a pristine snowfield with a single set of footprints which I realized were mine. When I asked for more clarity I was guided with "walk your talk with purity of spirit". I reflected that the snow was so pure and had not been stepped upon before – no-one else had trodden that path before, so I had to continue walking in purity. Another dream was quite significant: of being heavily pregnant, riding a horse. Seeing as horses can represent personal power, I felt this signified the birth of newly found power for me, especially as the next phase of the dream contained a seed tray with old compost, which then was falling into a beautiful tray as the compost seemed to take on new energy and tiny seedlings appeared to be growing in the newly energized environment. I took this to portend new growth in my being. I was also surrounded by beautiful special horses that I exchanged breath with. I couldn't get clear pictures of the individual horses, but I knew it was a real privilege to meet them. The meaning of the dream became clear when I met the wild horses in South Africa, who I will introduce to you in the next chapter!

The final dream was rather odd. I was somewhere desolate and I needed a lift. Then, I was on board a train and there was a fallen tree on the track. The next minute I seemed to be up in the tree and then falling out of it! I was sure I was going to be killed or at least very badly injured. As I landed, I found myself in a very sacred place. I gathered a few people to tell them about it and then suddenly there were loads of people listening to me. I then began to levitate, first vertically, then horizontally. I was telling them about honouring Isis, Hathor and Sekhmet. Afterwards I apologized and said I hoped it hadn't freaked too many people out, but no-one seemed to be upset by it! I felt all these dreams were quite auspicious about my future growth with new beginnings and positive change in my life and soul purpose, so I looked forward to what might unfold.

Swimming with Rajan was an unforgettable experience

Sacred white lions, seals, southern right whales, wild horses and unicorns

"We must embrace the original view of creation, that everything around us is part of one great and interconnected whole."
—Credo Mutwa

Two years before, I had been sent a website address telling me about sacred white lions that had been released back into the wild. When I looked at it, I was met by the most fantastic gaze from light blue eyes in the head of a huge male lion with a superimposed Ankh on his third eye. As I stared at him, I tingled from head to toe and felt that my socks were about to be blown off by the energy of the lion's stare. I vowed that one day I would go to South Africa and meet him as he called me to join him and learn the white lion wisdom. I didn't know how that would ever come about, but I joined the mailing list for news of the pride's progress. With house moves and general stresses and strains of normal family life, the prospect of ever getting to meet the lion in person seemed to fade. It sank into my memory as perhaps just another pipe dream. However, two years later I received another email in the form of an invitation. I still don't know exactly why I had been asked as I wasn't yet a member of the trust. I was invited to be part of an inner circle group to journey into the heartland of the white lions. When I read the proposed itinerary, I could hardly contain myself! The words lions, Ancient Egypt and unicorns, all in one sentence, set me in a fever of excitement. Once again, I felt a raiding of my adventure fund coming on. I emailed back straight away asking if I could come, if there was still a place for me, and couldn't wait to receive my answer. I checked on the prices of flights to Johannesburg and managed to find a really good flight from my local airport, which would change at Paris and then I would have to catch the tiny plane to Hoedspruit, a small airfield in the Kruger National Park. The names conjured up wonderful images in my mind as I awaited the moment when I could book and travel in the few weeks that remained before the journey date. I received an email and read with baited breath as I was told that there was a place for me. The trip was only a few weeks away so I booked all my flights there and then in a flurry of excitement.

The day before I was due to fly, it had been arranged that I was to have a cranio-sacral treatment with a lovely friend of mine called Anna. Our previous sessions had always resulted in all kinds of past life injuries, emotional and physical, coming up to be released and resolved. This session was rather different. As Anna worked on my body, I began to get a vision of a large stone room and I was kneeling on the stone floor. Around me in a semi-circle formation were what appeared to be Knights Templar. I could see their armour and chain mail, and they had large swords held upright to their faces. They were asking me if I would agree to the task they were bestowing on me. It was a weighty honour and I felt I had to fully commit to their behest, as it was not to be taken lightly. However, it also felt like I was so honoured to be asked and I could hardly refuse. So I agreed, not knowing quite what it was they were asking me to commit to. I just knew I had to. As I agreed, they formed a circle around me and I counted 12 knights. As they surrounded me, I heard the heavy tread of their armoured feet on the stone as they solemnly lowered their swords in my direction. Suddenly, the room seemed to fill up with other knights and a crowd of people who seemed to be asking me questions as though they expected me to know the answers to the whereabouts of sacred treasure and suchlike. I felt that these secrets should not be divulged, so I refused to tell them anything, even though I felt they had promised me great riches in exchange for my knowledge. With that, the crowd disappeared and the 12 knights remained around me. It seemed that I had passed a test and they then proceeded to 'knight' me with their swords, dubbing me a speaker of the truth and a truth seeker. I still didn't know what this might entail and made no connections to my ensuing journey to the white lions. As I came back from my vision, blinking at Anna, she said that my body had been changing energetically and she had felt that a lot had been going on! I told her of my vision and we both agreed that it felt very important and auspicious, and I hoped that I would in time understand my mission, which I had not accepted lightly.

I drove to Bristol airport and caught the flight to Paris, where I would change for Johannesburg. Eventually we landed in Johannesburg and I waited for my connecting flight to the Kruger. Afrikaans accents filled my ears in the hustle and bustle of the airport. I saw a young woman with long wavy brown hair. I don't know quite why she caught my notice, but she was obviously waiting for the same flight, along with some Americans who boarded our bus that took us to the small plane. They chatted to the woman about the safari they were going on and they asked her what she was doing. I felt sure she was going to the white lions, although I don't know why as she said nothing about them, so I thought I must have been mistaken.

I soon had my first glimpses of South Africa from the plane. Strange shapes of crop irrigation circles whizzed past underneath us. Then we were flying over the bush and I could make out the ochre-coloured, dusty tracks beneath us. There was lots of jovial chat from the Americans who were in high spirits. I couldn't see where the woman I had been interested in had sat, but when we alighted from the plane my intuition proved to be correct. Waiting just outside the tiny airport was Jason, holding the White Lion Trust placard. I marched up to him, announcing myself and right behind me was my suspect, called Larissa. We just laughed at each other, as we both admitted that we just knew we would both be going to the white lions! Jason Turner had met us with the Trust's land rover, emblazoned with the same image that had stared out at me, years before, from my computer screen. He is a lion ecologist with ten years of research on the behaviour and predatory nature of Timbavati's lions, and was to explain his vital work later. We were to meet the others at a local bar and then convoy into the sacred land of Timbavati, the home of the white lion pride. We met the other inner circle group at the bar and followed each other in our vehicles into the reserve, using the telemetry equipment to make sure the lions were not too close as we had to open and shut the large gates in the compound fencing. We listened intently for any 'bleeps' that might signal the proximity of the radio collars that the lions were wearing, so their safety could be monitored. Larissa and I began to feel very emotional, and I could feel the lion energy building in my solar plexus. Larissa had tears streaming down her face with the sheer emotion of being in the white lion energy field. We glimpsed warthogs charging through the undergrowth and wildebeests cavorted across our track. These were all images that had filled my television screen from documentaries I'd avidly consumed in my love of wildlife. Not for the first time, I had to pinch myself to make sure it wasn't all a wonderful dream. We finally arrived at the camp and were met by a lady called Teri – I also found out that she lived very close to me in the southwest of England and knew some clients of mine. Strange that we had to go all the way to South Africa to meet each other! She was volunteering there, and so was on gate duty. We were allotted our homes for the next few days, beautifully-coloured, thatched mud rondawels. I was to share with a Polish girl who had travelled all the way from Australia to be there, just to spend a few days with the white lions. The group was wonderful and we all felt a deep connection in a kindred calling to connect with the sacred star beings who were called the 'Children of the Sun God'. We were presented with a high tea of chocolate cake and muffins and then allowed to climb into the land rover to go to the rooftop hideout to see if we could find the lions and watch the sunset over the bush. We didn't see the lions that night, but we felt their presence, and the smells and sounds of the bush intoxicated us. There was a short lecture about the work the Trust was doing and I was horrified to learn about the brutal trade in the canned hunting industry, where both tawny and white lions were being bred to be chosen and killed by trophy hunters. They were advertized and chosen on the internet, and then shot in small compounds where the animal had no chance of escape. There were huge amounts of money involved and so it was a very profitable business. Unfortunately all the white lions had been poached in the wild and most of those bred in captivity either ended up being shot or in breeding programmes, their offspring suffering a terrible fate. The lions had no official protection, so Jason was desperately trying to isolate the white genetic marker to prove they were a distinct sub-species and not just freaks of nature. They are not albino and the Timbavati region is the only place in the world where the white lions had been born wild to tawny lions with the white gene. Currently there is no law to stop anyone killing the sacred beasts. A wonderful woman called Linda Tucker, and Jason, were fighting to get them protected status and, against great odds, were responsible for re-establishing a lineage of white lions back in the wild after many years.

I had an interesting night, being awakened at three o'clock in the morning by music blaring out of my roommate's mobile phone. We also had a very noisy metal bolt on our door that had to be creaked open in order to visit the toilet in the middle of the night. There was no quiet way to operate the bolt, so I wondered if I would get any sleep. I was, I admit, almost too excited, but I needed to catch up on sleep. Anyway, we awoke full of excitement for our first encounter to meet the 'royal pride'. We scrambled into the jeep and we made our way out into the bush. The lions were monitored at least three times a day to make sure they were safe from poachers. I had taken a notebook to scribble down anything that I might intuit from the lions. Linda was holding the tracking equipment out of the window as she explained that there was a lioness and her three large cubs in the location. The male lion, the father of the cubs, had been spotted elsewhere. We listened, straining our ears, for the telltale signal of a bleep on the telemetry screen. Suddenly they were upon us, walking right next to the land rover. They nonchalantly gazed at us as they padded past. One of the male cubs seemed a little slower than his brother and he hung back a bit. As I stared in admiration at the beautiful lioness who was called Zihra, I was amazed to 'see' stars tumbling down above her head. As the starlight cascaded down, words filled my head as I frantically scribbled. Linda had told us of her heartache in her efforts to rescue the iconic lioness Marah, who was born in a terrible trophy hunting camp. Marah's mother had been stolen from Timbavati and Marah's father had been stolen from a South African zoo. As foretold by the African elders, Marah was born on Christmas Day in a place called Bethlehem, which ironically is the black heart of South Africa's canned hunting industry. Linda's task was to rescue this sacred lioness and return her to her natural and spiritual homelands of the Timbavati region, meaning 'place where the starlions came down'. Linda was trained by African elders, including lion shaman Maria Khosa and medicine man Credo Mutwa. She included this sacred knowledge in the book, *The Mystery of the White Lions*. As the lioness of prophecy, Marah's name was given by the African elders, meaning 'Mother of the Sun God'. Rather like the return of the white buffalo for the Native Americans, the Africans believed that if the white lion returned to their heartland, Africa could be healed from war and disaster. After four years of battle, Linda managed to rescue Marah with her three cubs from brutal captivity. With the help of a generous benefactor, Linda managed to secure vast tracks of sacred heritage lands for Marah's return to the wild. Against all the odds, Marah managed to hunt within weeks of her release and was able to provide successfully for her fast growing family in her natural endemic habitat.

When she unexpectedly passed into spirit a year later, while doing what she did best – hunting and providing for her cubs – it was a tragic blow for the project. Marah was like a sister or mother to Linda, but fortunately Linda's training helped her recognize that Marah was still guiding the project from the ancestral realms, and fortunately Marah's cubs had become good hunters, so they were able to survive and hunt on their own.

Through her training, Linda has the ability to communicate with Marah directly, but what I received corroborated the information Linda herself had been getting.

Linda fought back the tears as I read out the words that I had received in my head from the tumbling star energy. I was told that this was how Marah was going to connect with us. Through her daughter Zihra, I was able to jot down Marah's words. Linda had received a message that Marah reigned in 144 galaxies. Amazingly, I received the same message. But although Marah was a supreme celestial being, her loving focus remained on the earth, and critical events taking place here. She said:

"I am here, tell Linda to release her sadness like a flower opening in her heart, and
allowing it to breathe out. I have left my legacy and all is in place.
My granddaughter will take awareness to new heights and she will anchor the
star energy further as I direct the galaxies. This will coincide with the 2012
changes. All is in divine and perfect order. All is well."

From then on, every time I saw Zihra the stars would tumble down and I knew that Marah was close from spirit. Like their mother, Marah's cubs have names that associated with the sun. Zihra, and her brother's names Regeus and Letaba, all mean the 'first ray of sunshine' in different languages. Zihra's daughter of whom Marah spoke was called Nebu, which means pure gold. This little girl, according to Marah, had a very important role to play in the future of the planet. Her brothers, Matsieng (meaning Orion) and Zukara (meaning Great Spirit of Ra), were magnificent. However Matsieng, so I was told by Zukara, struggled with the pulse of the electric fence, which enforced the safety of the lions on the reserve boundaries. It seemed little Matsieng was very sensitive to the electromagnetic currents, and I was told that it often gave him a headache! He lay with his back towards me, so I gave him some balancing healing energy as best I could and hoped that it might help in some way.

I visualized working up through his chakras. He suddenly got up and gave a lovely stretch, which I hoped showed that he had received some healing and rebalancing. Zukara seemed quite happy with my efforts. Linda told us not to stare into their eyes as it would be disrespectful – we certainly felt like they were giving us an audience from their royal domain. Seeing them so close made me feel very humble to be in their presence. We all felt our hearts were about to explode as we saw the whole family unite as the huge male Mandla strolled across the track in the distance. This was the lion who had called me to come to South Africa. I then learned the truth behind this most powerful being. He had been offered as the highest income-earning trophy, before Linda and Jason managed to rescue him from the canned hunting industry under terrible duress. He had spent his entire life caged, but now he was wild and free. And what's more, he had sired Zihra's litter of beautiful children – Marah's grandchildren.

Even in the distance I could see how huge he was, but we had to wait until the next day to meet our royal sovereign properly. A cursory, crystal blue-eyed glance in our direction, and then he was lost in the bush. It's hard to believe how white lions can be so well camouflaged, but they seemed to melt into the undergrowth and leave us in a spin of hushed fervour.

On the next encounter, we were lucky enough to follow the huge paw prints in the orange dust and find Mandla lying on his back. He had obviously feasted well in the night, as his engorged, distended belly showed. His repose was not quite so regal, with his mighty limbs spread akimbo, his jowl lolling in the warmth of the morning sun. He seemed disinclined to engage with us after his busy night, but I managed to ask him a few questions, which he was gracious enough to answer from his sleepy state. Linda had asked me to question him as to how he felt about the kills Zihra was making, and if he felt like making his own kills. He had killed a civet when he was released, but seemed to enjoy taking, literally, the lion's share from his mate's hard-won prey. He told me that he was busy when he slept, as he visited the 'star council' to converse in matters of great importance. Linda said that she had seen him appear to leave his body, so she was not surprised at his strange revelations. He also told me, when I asked him about his eating habits, that he loved the internal organs of large prey. He said he liked to take the 'life force' contained in the nutrients of the liver, kidneys and heart. He admitted that he was worried about the boundaries of the nearby reserves as there were lions that were not so respected and may be destined for the canned hunting industry. He was also tired from his exertions of protecting the pride from the neighbouring black-maned tawny lion, who had the audacity to make eyes at Zihra! All this effort took its toll and we felt it only proper that we should leave him to his slumber.

Our days in-between visiting the lions were filled with wonderful experiences, which included a lovely workshop, working with the healing properties and the power of positive thought on water, next to the cool Klaserie River that ran through the reserve. We also met in the wild fig forests for a picnic brunch, after a soul walk of silent tracking with a Shangaan guide. We had spotted a civet latrine and I became quite expert at identifying porcupine poo!

We lay in meditation after lunch beneath the tree canopies with the sound of the gentle river flowing past. I managed to lie on a huge thorn that pierced deep into my thigh. Although it bled and was quite painful, I felt that, symbolically, I had to leave my DNA as my blood dripped onto the forest floor in this sacred place, and that it was somehow important as part of my commitment to the white lions and the planet. The area lies on the Nile meridian and so connects with the sacred energy of the great Sphinx in Ancient Egypt and the Siriun prophecy that there would be the coming of a golden age, when the white lion walked free once more. On the first morning of our stay we had made a mission statement about our commitment to the white lions. It only dawned on me later that perhaps this was the task I had agreed to undertake with the knights. I stated that I was to be the voice of truth for the animals, using my interspecies communication skills. It would be my mission to convey the messages from the planet's creatures in the best way I could. I pondered about there being 12 knights, as there were only seven of us in our inner circle group, but I knew that all would become clear in due course.

We had a wonderful encounter with Mandla that evening. We had been tracking him with the telemetry, and eventually found him in repose again, sleeping off a belly full of a poor unfortunate wildebeest. Drawing closer to him, and trying not to disturb him, I sent out waves of love from my heart to his, thanking him for allowing us to visit. I hadn't heard him roar very loudly – only in the distance as I felt he patrolled our camp at night. So I asked him if I could hear his royal voice before I left his heartland. We were just about to start the engine of the jeep, as he seemed deep in slumber, when suddenly he sat up, turned to us and gave a huge yawn. This turned into the most earth-shattering roar. His saliva and breath roared out between enormous jaws and his huge razor-sharp teeth glinted in the sunlight. The sheer volume and power of his roars brought up quite primordial feelings of fear that was very humbling. We had knelt on the floor of the enclosed jeep so that we could get a better view of him through the windows; it felt like every bone in our body was being shaken by the magnitude of his power. There was complete silence in the jeep as we listened in awe! It felt only right that we should kneel in his presence! Finally, he ceased his serenading and slumped back into the common posture of a sleepy lion. I thanked him with all my heart for the gift he had bestowed upon us and I shall never forget the ear-splitting sound that permeated our very being. That last night, as I lay in my rondavel, he continued his monitoring of the camp, surveying his domain. His haunting roars echoed around the Boma and our fragile huts. Far from being scared by his proximity, I felt that he was protecting us as we were part of his sovereignty, and I hoped he felt we were loyal subjects! I lay in my bed listening in wonder to his fantastic sounds.

We were all a bit sleepy on our last morning before we left the camp to journey to the wild horses. There was one last visit to the royal family.

I was asked if I thought I could connect with the young male cubs, Matsieng and Zukara, to ask them not to join us in the open top jeep, as apparently they could be a little curious and could I ask them to please stay on the ground! Linda asked me if I thought the group would remain calm if the cubs (who were quite large now) became inquisitive. I felt the group had gelled together incredibly well, with total respect and love for the lions. I knew everyone would give out the right energy, so we set out on our final encounter with mixed feelings. We were all excited at the prospect of meeting the wild horses and discovering the unicorn portals, but leaving the lions physically was quite a wrench. However, I think all of us vowed to return as soon as we could, and we knew that we could connect with them energetically whenever we wanted. There was nothing quite like seeing them up close in their natural environment. So Jason drove us through the bush along the many meandering dusty tracks that criss-crossed the land. We spotted some enormous Eland bulls on our way and I got the message that they represented power, their huge twisted horns towering upwards to the cool blue sky. Vultures fluttered in the branches above us and warthogs dashed out with tails erect in their rather comical gait. Impala stared at us from a distance and then danced off into the distant bush.

We finally found Zihra and the cubs, lazing in the bushes with distended tummies and it was great to see how well they were surviving by their own devices. Once again as I looked at the beautiful face of Zihra, I saw the tumbling stars that indicated the proximity of Marah's energy. Zihra told me that Marah taught her to 'feel' her prey by connecting to all the earth's vibrations---as though she could just use her huge paws to feel the vibration and this would lead her to her prey. She told me she was teaching this to her cubs, but that Matsieng became confused at times, because of the electric currents and that it threw him off-balance occasionally. I hoped that some of my balancing and visualized protection might help him a little. As the lions seemed very sleepy, we decided to move off and try and find Mandla who was absent from the group. Just as we started the engine, Zihra sat up and they all started to come towards us. We all felt that they wanted to tell us something, but Jason thought it expedient to move away as he didn't want them to get too used to following the vehicle that invaded their privacy. We sadly stared back at the beautiful creatures who were trotting, ears pricked, behind us. As the jeep sped away, we left them behind. We shared Jason's concerns to protect their wilderness and freedom, but at the same time we all felt that there were things left unsaid that we needed to hear from them. We all tried to consume as many images as possible to store forever in our hearts, as we felt that it might be the last time we ever saw them. So we longingly craned our heads to capture the last fading glimpses of the pride. We moaned at poor Jason for not allowing us to engage one last time with them, but of course we had to bow to his better judgement as he carried huge responsibility on his shoulders for their safety and wellbeing in the wild. But we all secretly hoped we'd somehow see them again, even if it meant returning some day!

Then we set our intention on finding Mandla for one last audience with his royal highness. We had some difficulty locating him, and nearly came to grief in a dry river bed when the wheels of the jeep became bogged down in the soft earth. It wasn't really prudent to consider getting out and pushing with lions in the area, so we rocked backwards and forwards, until eventually the wheels gripped the ground. The bleeps of the telemetry betrayed Mandla's location and this time we found him sitting erect, gazing into the distance as though trying to spot something in his distant vision. We couldn't get over just how huge he was, his massive paws were like dinner plates and his magnificent mane was caressed by a soft breeze. I asked him about the lion/unicorn connection. In most heraldry they seemed to always be in combative mode, either side of a coat of arms, both rearing as if in attack. He said this was symbolic of 'myth, mystery and magic' and when the lion and the unicorn united it would portend a symbiosis of perfect planetary harmony. I couldn't wait then to hear the unicorn's version of their vision for planetary union and peace. As I was busy scribbling down his words of wisdom, I suddenly got a big nudge in the ribs from one of my new friends in the group. We turned to see Zihra and the youngsters race up behind us and throw themselves into a loving embrace of their father and mate, Mandla. They had returned to us! Seeing the love for each other in their tenderest of greetings was so beautiful. They rubbed cheeks in greeting, which reminded me of my leonine encounter in the Sphinx village! It was obvious how much they loved each other as a family as they purred and collapsed on each other in a bundle of liony love. It was a privilege to witness their family interaction. It had taken us quite some time to find Mandla, and it seemed the rest of the family had effortlessly travelled through the bush to find their missing member, just moments behind us. We were so pleased to see them again and to know that we had just one more chance of connecting with them in the physical. They all stood and began to file past, right next to the jeep. We all visualized sending out unconditional love from our heart centres and the biggest vote of thanks we could muster. The young boys did glance curiously in our direction as they filed past, and I 'told' them that I was so glad they were safe and enjoying their freedom in the wild. Respecting Jason's caution, I intimated that they really didn't want to get involved with the machinations of man and his machines. They seemed to accept this, as they nonchalantly strode past, returning their gaze to the bush. Their penetrating stare had bored into our very souls. Just as we thought they were all about to leave, little Nebu lay down right next to us as the others removed themselves from sight. It was very uncharacteristic for the little lioness to do this, but then I felt Marah's energy coming through again. They seemed to be discussing the momentous role that Nebu had agreed upon, at a soul level, to undertake for the future of the planet. I visualized wrapping her in protective light and thanked her for her courage and commitment to planetary healing, such an important role for one small lioness, ably guided by her grandmother Marah from spirit. She then stood up, stretched, and padded out of sight. We all felt incredibly blessed to have been in her company, and what a fitting finale to these few days of being immersed in the white lion energy. We all felt that Mandla and Marah would continue to influence our lives, and we all vowed to find a way to return some day, but in the meantime, I have photographic portraits of them both in my healing room at home, and feel their presence whenever I need to be 'lion-hearted'. See the last chapter for the 'lion heart' meditation they gave me, which helps me maintain their strength in my being, and to give strength to others, both animals and humans.

"Be lion-hearted in your endeavours, be strong in your protection, know that we are with you, and let our strength be your guide."
—Shaaksti, my male lion guide

The wild horses and unicorns of the Kaapse Hoope

Linda wanted to take us on a journey to meet the wild horses of a sacred site which is due south of Timbavati, because she'd been working on the ancient connection between the white lions and the unicorns. Leaving the lion camp, we sent out our goodbyes and thanks to the animals and the staff that had looked after us so well. As we left the white lion territory, we passed other reserves and saw huge giraffes towering up into the canopies, majestically searching for the tastiest leaves for their prehensile tongues, grasping the uppermost delicacies. As we sped along the road, I noticed a tiny grasshopper or cricket clinging to the windscreen where it joined the bonnet of the car. He seemed quite happy there as though he was enjoying his journey. We stopped for petrol, and I waited in the car, as others popped into the small filing station to buy some water and snacks. I took the opportunity to see if the tenacious insect had something to say to me. He said he was glad that I had finally asked him to speak. He'd clung on for many miles until we'd bothered to ask him for his words of wisdom! Rather reminiscent of the flies and the cockroach, he had that same serious expression that what he was going to impart was of great import. He was staring at me, waving his antennae, as though to hammer his message home. He said "Great change is coming". This felt like a very positive statement and I thanked him for his perseverance and apologized once again for being a mere simple human, who took a while to understand how important the messages from the animal kingdom were. He seemed pleased that I had at last listened and then leapt into the air, and was gone. When everyone came back I told them about our extra passenger's pearl of wisdom, and we all speculated as to what this might mean, and how auspicious that we were on our way to find the unicorns!

We travelled through countryside that was much more verdant than the landscape of the Timbavati region. We were hoping to visit the Dragon Mountains, but there was a lot of low lying cloud and we had been delayed in leaving the lion camp. Linda and Jason had had an important meeting with some officials who might be able to help with the white lion protected status, so we carried on until we reached the Kaapse Hoope, which is a massive escarpment. We were told that the view from the top of the escarpment was spectacular, but it was hard to see anything as the cloud and mist obscured everything but the landscape within a few yards of us. However, when we climbed up through the rocky terrain, we found the horses waiting for us. Apparently they could be elusive, but they seemed to be expecting us. The herd stood with ears pricked, looking intently at us, and far from seeming disturbed by our presence they all came closer as if to inspect our intentions and collective energy. There was a dun-coloured mare, who seemed to be an alpha mare of the herd and at her foot was the most beautiful dark bay foal. I was 'told' that this foal was a star being and was, rather like Nebu, to take the future of the horse/unicorn wisdom into 2012. I was given etheric blue crystal orbs, almost identical to the ones I had placed in the earth in Sedona. We all sat on the rocky ground and I placed the orbs into the earth. Linda played a Tibetan singing bowl as we sat in reverence in front of the horses, which came ever closer in their inspection of us. I felt that so many of the horses were Atlantean. I had come across only very few in the past that I felt had the genetic blueprint of the golden horses of Atlantis. I was amazed at there being so many, in fact a whole herd. This is hard to describe as it's a kind of just knowing. They are nearly all chestnut and have a curious whorl of hair on their third eye centres on their foreheads. The many chestnut horses of the herd seemed to hear my question, to which they replied:

> *"Yes we are the golden horses, we guard the unicorn portals.*
> *We feel the white lion presence within you. We thank you for*
> *coming to bring unity and healing to our land."*

The stallion came within a few feet of us as we sat before him. We all sent out love from our hearts and prayed that he would permit us to remain near his herd. He stood right in front of me and I felt very small, sitting with my eyes shut, as he seemed to scan our energy fields. I was aware that he could easily have shown aggression and we were in a potentially dangerous situation, as he scrutinized us. However as we showed the utmost respect and all of us visualized opening our hearts and expanding our love outwards, we hoped he could feel our loving intentions. The horses came closer and closer as we gently stood to leave. A freezing wind blew through us, and it started to drizzle with rain. The light was beginning to fade due to the low cloud and we realized that time had seemed to stand still, but it was now evident that evening was fast approaching. However the horses stood in front of us blocking our descent. They seemed resolute in keeping us there until we understood what they wanted us to do. My Polish friend was rather nervous of horses, and as she leaned against a stony outcrop, one of the young colts actually backed into her, leaning his back legs and rump, right against her body. Momentarily, I was a little alarmed, as he could have inflicted serious injury to her if he had lashed out, but it seemed that it was another tactic in pinning us to the mountain until we understood our mission! We asked them what they wanted and they asked us to return the next morning to work with the energies of specific places on the mountain. Linda, who had been there before, asked me to ask them which of her suggestions did they feel were the most important areas to focus on. They seemed keen for us to agree to go to a place that Linda called the star gate and then they said they would instruct us when we got there! Once this was agreed we all felt the unicorns surrounding us. The horses had formed a crescent shape in front of us, but the etheric unicorns seemed to envelop us all. There were many strange rock formations that looked like ossified animals, frozen in time, and we felt that somehow we would be able to help breathe new life into the imprisoned animals within. Once we all were committed to doing our best to help the next morning, the unicorns faded and the herd parted, allowing us safe passage down the mountain.

The magnificent Mandla

We had nothing to fear from the wild horses, but the light had really begun to fade. We hadn't thought of bringing any torches, as we hadn't anticipated staying on the mountain for so long. Climbing down was much harder than our previous ascent. The path was quite treacherous as we stumbled down in near darkness, trying not to slip on the rocks. I asked the horses for protection and immediately felt much safer, as though I could use their night vision to help me find the path. Gradually we saw twinkling lights of some houses in the distance, near where we had parked the cars. We were all quite exhausted and hungry too. Just as we were deliberating on whether we should go to a bar that we'd passed on our way to the mountain, we were approached by some rather inebriated young men. They said we should join them and that they'd come from a hotel just up the street that was 'really dead'. We thanked them for their invitation, but all felt that somewhere 'really dead' was just what we needed. The hotel was called the 'Silver Mist' and we thawed our shivering bodies in front of a roaring log fire.

We arrived at Linda's guest house around 11pm. It was so beautiful with its thatched courtyard and individual roundavels connected by the roof. I fell into my welcoming bed and dreamt of unicorns and lions all interacting in harmony with each other. Next morning we breakfasted on tea and muffins and made our way back to the escarpment, as promised. We hadn't seen how beautiful the grounds of the guest house were in the dark the night before, but we drove down a jacaranda tree-lined avenue, their beautiful lilac-blue flowers billowing gently in the breeze. It was still quite cloudy and not much warmer, but undeterred we made our way to the horses. There were quite a few grazing on the grass verge next to the road, but their presence was less evident on the mountain. We felt they were watching in the wings to see if we carried out the work they had instructed us to do. We started to climb up through the rocky outcrops, again being struck by the shapes that looked as if the Snow Queen had wreaked her havoc on living creatures, and frozen them in time. We were guided to turn left and right until we found what appeared to be a miniature Stonehenge formation, where someone had already laid flowers and apples in a ceremonial offering. We sat in a circle and chanted, calling in the energies of the unicorns and we felt them surround us. I was guided to let out the huge roars that seemed to be welling up inside me. It felt as though Mandla had stepped inside me and he was using me as some kind of conduit to give voice to the creation of the lion/unicorn unity. Rather like the roars that emanated out of me in Egypt, I sat with my eyes closed and let the sound come thundering out. I was shocked at how much volume and power roared out of me. It was an incredible moment as all of us gave voice to the healing mission of the white lions. We felt the vortexes open around us as the unicorns stepped through. We were then guided to move on and we all took our shoes and socks off to better connect to Mother Earth. Linda played the singing bowl again, as we continued the climb to our next sacred site. We reached what was called the Unicorn Point, which I intuited connected directly to the Isis Point in the Grand Canyon. A tiny yellow flower had got stuck between my toes and the other members of our group found flowers to throw onto the mammoth rock. It seemed to erupt from the fathomless depths of the escarpment, which was still shrouded in mist. I gently lifted the flower from my toes and threw it onto the rock. We were so overpowered by the energies there we all knelt down, and then I began to shake as I felt Marah come through from spirit. I was guided to speak some words that seemed to explain why she had decided to pass after all. I felt Sekhmet speak through me:

"Dearest Marah, may your roars ring through the cosmos, showering us with your love, showering us with starlight. Our deepest heartfelt gratitude for the sacrifice you made in order to bring unity to the earth, unifying the lion/unicorn connection at last to free all fear into the new paradigm."

We were all sobbing at the enormity of her sacrifice, as though she'd known she could perform much more healing work from spirit to facilitate the new awakenings for 2012. She said that once unity was complete all the ossified animals would be set free and come to life. We kept being told by the horses "There's one more place, there's one more place"! And then we were led to the star gate. We caressed and kissed the beautiful stone formation and sent out our prayers for unity for our planet. We laid yet more flowers with our prayers in this beautiful site. I was guided to place an enormous sun disc in the precipice to reflect the light of the unicorns out into the whole valley. After a while, we all felt a sense of completion and felt our work was done. No horses blocked our path as we jubilantly left the mountain. We felt they were satisfied with our deliberations and we all hoped that whatever we had achieved would play a small part in the planetary healing, so needed for all of our futures.

It was very sad saying goodbye to the group as we all went our different ways, having grown so close over the past few days and we had forged real friendships in the camaraderie of our efforts. We all felt sure we would meet again, so it was with a kind of knowing 'until the next time' as we hugged our farewells.

I was due to stay in an area about 40 minutes from Cape Town, as I had booked a trip to a lion sanctuary. So I boarded a flight from Nelspruit airport, back to Johannesburg and then on to Cape Town. I was given a lift to the airport and then caught the flight with the small plane to Johannesburg. We had a rather eventful journey as there was a lot of rough turbulence as we neared Johannesburg. We got caught up in a thunderstorm with violent lightning which was a little worrying! We were delayed in the airport due to the weather, but eventually left for Cape Town, and as we flew in over the myriad of twinkling lights, I wondered what adventures awaited me. My biggest fear was driving a hire car, which I had never done on my own in a strange country. At least I could drive on the same side of the road, but I had heard scary stories of female tourists being hijacked, robbed and perhaps worse. However, the kind people I was to stay with on my first night, and who had collected me from the airport, assured me it was the best thing for me to have my freedom

The beautiful princess Nebu

and get around to see more South African animals and sites. I thought then, as I had travelled so far, I might as well experience as much as possible in order to learn more from the wildlife there. My first night was in Noerdhook, with a South African animal communicator called Wynter. She was running the course at a lion sanctuary in two days time which I was keen to experience. She also worked alongside Baboon Matters, who monitored the wild baboons that roamed the area. We were to sleep in tents in the middle of the lions, and communicate with the very troubled lions that had been rescued from terrible conditions around the world. There, they would receive loving care, respect and protection for the rest of their lives.

I had a lovely lie-in on my first morning there and then went to collect my hire car. I also wanted to visit the Southern Right whales that were migrating off the southern tip of South Africa. I had a map but I was a little worried about driving the two-hour journey there on my own. I was then booked into what I can only describe as the best little B & B establishment you could ever wish for. It was called "The House at Pooh Corner" and I was given 'Roo's Room'. Kathy, the proprietor, was the epitome of kindness and served up the best breakfasts I have ever tasted for my dairy, citrus and wheat allergy limited diet. I had severe withdrawal symptoms when I went home. It was such a gorgeous location and I missed her innovative culinary wonders!

I went to collect Wynter for our journey to Drakenstein Lion Sanctuary and she drove through on the busy freeways as I tried to get my bearings around the area. On entering the sanctuary, you began to get a sense of the lion energy, which seemed to make your solar plexus flip and your heart skip a few beats. They were such magnificent beasts and the idea of anyone not respecting and revering these regal creatures mystified me. Most had come from foreign circuses, where they had been caged in tiny trailers in terrible conditions, or rescued from the dreadful fate of the canned hunting industry. They had 27 lions at the sanctuary, mostly male. They were planning several more rescues at that time, and were battling with the red tape involved in the rescue of lions from destinations such as France and Romania. They had one white lion female cub who had been introduced to two orphan tawny cubs. She was having trouble fitting in, being still very stressed at the separation from her mother and the death of her litter sister that the sanctuary had tried in vain to save. They were taken away far too young from their mother, so that she would come into oestrus again and then would produce another litter – more fodder for the canned hunting. The cubs had not been fed correctly so only one cub survived. The white cub was called Ziyanda and her spirit sister was called Zintle. I tuned into them both and received the following information; Zintle was just too fey for this world and not strong enough for the physical existence. Ziyanda has to take on the physical role even though she finds it very difficult. Zintle just didn't have the strength of physical life-force. Her role was to exist in the physical, just for a short time, to support Ziyanda enough for her to survive and carry the message of the white lions forward. She connects with Marah in spirit to work in union as a pure energy light being. She can go where she is needed to give support. She has a much stronger energy in spirit and if Ziyanda can work at tuning into her more, as she will when she gets more mature, she will receive so much strength from the white lion consciousness. Ziyanda is too worried at present about fitting in and finding her physical place in the hierarchy. She is not quite able at present to connect to her spiritual role. When she sleeps, Zintle is more able to connect, but when she is awake, she becomes too distracted. This made sense and I remembered the role of the captive dolphins in the Dominican Republic, affecting the tourists on a deep level. Drakenstein was drawing many tourists now and a white lion was a big attraction, so Ziyanda would be able to affect many more people in this way. We chatted to quite a few of the lions before our stay in the camp in the middle of the campus. It was a very windy night and I shared a tent with a beautiful Canadian fashion model who was passionate about big cats. It was a very cold night as it was so blustery and we were supplied with welcome hot water bottles to cuddle. It was a little alarming to feel the lions so close as they roared all night, right next to our tents. At any moment, you felt that a huge, maned intruder would rip the canvas with his giant claws and find us huddling within. It was an amazing experience, but there's something very primordial about hearing the roaring that vibrated around the valley as they all vied for the territory. It brought up a lot of instinctive fear as I thought about the huge cave lions and sabre tooth tigers that prehistoric man would have had to contend with. However, my new friend and I just lay in our camp beds, and relished the opportunity to share the night with so many lions.

We conversed with some more of the lions and I was thrilled to tune into a conversation between a very traumatized and fierce lioness called Simba, and the young daughter or one of our group. Simba was extremely dangerous and had a very poor opinion of man. At 18 years old, she was the oldest rescue case there. She was in season and one of the pair of male lions in the enclosure opposite her was in lust with her. Every time we passed by on our way to the tents and momentarily blocked the view of the object of his desire, he would fly at the wire with terrifying ferocity. Simba was so angry at the disrespect she had received and also felt the anguish of all the other lions that had come and gone from the sanctuary. I sat on the ground next to her fence and overheard the conversation she was having with the young teenager. She was saying how grateful she was that the 'young' one had taken time to ask her opinions. Simba flatly refused to 'talk' to anyone else and ignored all the visitors, who tried to engage with her. She said:

"All is not lost for mankind if the young are open to understanding my pain. They are the ones to take the lion's message for the need to respect them as a symbol of respecting Africa and the planet."

I felt this was a very important exchange and the young girl told Simba that she would spread her wise words with the school friends, to raise awareness of the plight of lions, and that if man can disrespect the king of beasts so carelessly, it was indicative of the lack of respect for the planet. A lovely lion called Samson showed me his previous life in a circus where he had been trained with meat on a metal stick. He was also poked with the stick and his paws had terrible sores from the faeces and urine he was forced to live in, inside his tiny filthy cage. He said he loved the feel of the soft grass in his new home and liked the smell of the flowers. He still felt as though he was carrying a lot of anger, understandably, so I worked to try and help him release his trauma. I hoped that I might have helped him enjoy his new life a little bit more. We left the sanctuary, feeling that a least a few lucky lions were now being well cared for, for the rest of their lives. I try to keep in touch with the sanctuary and send funds when I can to help with the new rescues.

Wynter asked if I would like to meet some baboons, so we met at the Baboon Matters office, who try and monitor the local troop of baboons that were making a nuisance of themselves around the townships. They employed local people to act as wardens to chase the them away from anywhere where they were running into trouble and occasionally being shot. We found the troop in some trees on the outskirts of town and we sat underneath, trying to send our love and to ask them to keep safe. The huge male was bombarding us with huge pine cones – we didn't take it personally, he was throwing them down to feed the rest of his troop, and we had chosen an unwise place to sit for our conversation! The troop surrounded us as they grabbed the cones and then suddenly they dropped everything and took off, with a bark from the male. Much to the consternation of the wardens, the troop descended upon some houses on the periphery of the town. They raced across the roofs, shimmying down the drain pipes like some comical firemen, leaping onto a carousel washing line and plucking off the washing as the pegs snapped and flew through the air. A youngster plucked a denim skirt and went dashing up the pipes and over the roof tops. The poor lady who owned the washing line came to retrieve her washing, which had disappeared. It was amusing to see their antics, but it made them very unpopular with the residents. Baboon Matters worked hard to raise funds to employ more wardens to prevent their troublesome behaviour, so that human and baboon could co-exist. It was their territory after all and we were infringing on it as the human population grew. It had been interesting to be at ground level with the families and observe how they interacted with each other, as the babies clung to their mothers who tenderly cared for their young. I hadn't really felt that attracted to baboons before, but they showed such devotion to their families and it was yet another lesson for me to appreciate about the importance of the diversity of the animal kingdom.

I also met some other rather comical characters on one of my brave solo outings in the hire car. I drove to a nearby town called Simonstown and a beach called Boulder Beach because of the enormous boulders that looked as though a giant had failed at skimming the huge stones into the water, and they now lay scattered around the shoreline. There was a large colony of penguins and I wanted to see if I could connect with them and find out what they might say. I parked the car and walked down to the viewing area near the beach. Although they were so graceful in the sea, on land they were slightly less nimble as they hopped from rock to rock rather unsteadily on their webbed feet. I came across a rather sad looking individual, who seemed to be glaring at a very fat penguin sunning himself in front of him. I tried to ask the penguin why he looked so sad and he 'showed' me a video-like clip in my mind of them being in the sea and hunting fish. The sad penguin showed me that he'd had a lovely fish right in his sights and the greedy perpetrator had snatched the fish from underneath his nose (or beak!). The poor penguin had gone hungry, as he hadn't managed to catch any other fish that day. The smug expression on his rotund opponent summed it all up. I tried to send out love to them, and I hoped that he would have a better catch next time. Again, it was fascinating to witness the dynamics within the colony.

The next day, my new friend from the white lion camp, Larissa, arrived at Pooh Corner, as I had invited her to come with me to meet the whales. I was happy to drive – it was just great having her there as navigator, we were both excited at the prospect of seeing the migrating whales. The coastal scenery was spectacular and reminded me of the roads I had seen in a film about Monte Carlo. It was simply breathtaking as the mountains met the sea, with sheer drops into the ocean, down the sides of the roads. We arrived at Hermanus bay at three o'clock; we had about an hour until the time when the whales would show themselves as they rested in the bay. We climbed out on the rather precarious rocky promontory to get a good view of the whales as they swam past. There were seals frolicking in the waves as they crashed into the rocks. I was amazed that they weren't smashed against the craggy shore, but they seemed to just appear again unscathed, almost mocking our concern. It felt like they were the 'warm up' act as we waited in anticipation for the whales to show themselves. They tossed bits of seaweed and fish, into the air and then cavorted through the waves. This is what they said as I tuned into their antics:

"We bring joy and levity as we frolic in the waves. We show you the art of play and the need for laughter as we make you smile. We mimic the whales, fluking as we dive. We focus your attention on the beauty and the power of the sea, as we effortlessly dodge the crashing waves that dash against the rocks. We are so adept, you marvel at our prowess to be at one with the waves. We introduce you to the seriousness of the whale's message in a light hearted manner as we fix your gaze on the surface of the sea. Our small dark shapes set the precedent for the larger ones that carry the song of the sea. We entertain while you await their presence. We are happy to do this as we infect you with our fun! Be joyous in the world, spread our joy and appreciation for all life, as it is wondrous, yet fragile — each living cell, a marvel to be cherished."

What words of wisdom from a seemingly unlikely source! I hurriedly scribbled down their words as a commotion spread amongst the small crowd who had joined us on the promontory. Right on cue, in the distance, several whales could be seen blowing their distinctive double spurts. We could see them breaching and as they came nearer, a mother and calf drifted slowly by, spy hopping as they peaked at the crowd that had been awaiting their arrival. Others were fluking in the distance as their enormous tails lifted momentarily out it the water, only to disappear into the depths of the ocean. I sent out a cord of love from my heart to connect to the whale's heart, as the big cow brought her baby close to the shore. This is what she said as she slowly passed by:

"Our journey is long and dangerous especially for our little ones. We sing our

song of love for mother Gaia. We sing our song to bring balance to ourselves and the earth. Mankind has brought discordance and death to so many of us over time, but we still choose to bring healing and the recognition of the need to love all creation. All is divine and contains divinity within. The echoes of our song's vibrations resonate that message through each water molecule of the sea, which splashes and sprays this message onto the rocks and shores, infusing the land with our song's energy and clarion call to all."

I felt her words were so poignant and beautiful, and I thanked her from the bottom of my heart as she guided her baby further out to sea. I prayed they would be safe and reach the better feeding grounds they were searching for.

I had also received an amazing email from a woman called Sharon, who had been part of the Inner Circle group. She had received channelled information for all of us as to our future roles to connect with the white lions and how that would help us with planetary healing. I was amazed when I counted the number of people included in the messages as there were 12 others. Sharon's guide, Serapis Bey, had messages for Linda, Jason and other members of the team. It suddenly dawned on me that these were the 12 that I was to work with – these were my knights! This is the message:

Message for Madeleine

Your work as animal communicator is extremely valuable and holds a special significance for the white lions and leopards, for you will be called upon often in the future to interact with the white lions to convey their messages to the Inner Circle group. You will be a channel of communication for them and other animals to use as a means of communicating their needs and feelings to the humans who are enforcing control of their habitats. The animals also have a special message regarding the waterways for this planet and this will come through to you in a moment of quiet meditation. This will have profound significance for the entire planet and you will know it and understand its powerful message when it happens. This message must also be conveyed in your future writings to be included in your new book, since it is destined to have a major impact for life in general. You must link it to Dr Emoto's work with water and also to Sharon's work with salt pyramids and water (with their permission), since there is a combined message in this for all. Work closely with the great White Lion King — for he holds all the clues — when your intent is sincere and you are ready, he will reveal all, but not until the time is fully right (which can only be after Larissa's re-activation of the light tube through Zimbabwe). In the meantime, assist the group with sending light energy as often as you can and invite the animals to partake regularly in your meditation sessions, especially when you set the intent to connect whilst in meditation with the Inner Circle as there is much guidance to be learned from the animals, which will benefit the earth as a whole. Stay grounded and in your heart energy as you are fully on track — you are dearly loved and held in great awe for the work you are doing by all on this side of the veil. Not only do you have an entourage of angels and light beings, but armies of animals in the spirit world all anxious to help and support you in your role in this lesson. You are divinely guided — be careful though not to fall into the trap of allowing the ego to take control. Keep your line of channel clear and open and ask politely that your ego steps aside so that the truth in the form of accurate messages from the Light can come through. Do not fall into the trap of feeling pressurized to do a reading for someone when the energy or the contact doesn't feel right. If you truly can't receive something, say so — you will be honoured for your integrity and the next time spirit will reward you with a wonderfully accurate message. Resist the temptation to give messages when you feel tired or your energy might not be fully aligned. We know it is in your nature to want to please everyone and we commend you for this, but there may be times when your physical energy may not be fully in tune and your receptors are not functioning to their full capacity. It is at times like this that you must resist the temptation to give a message if you have the slightest doubt that it might be influenced by your ego. You understand, don't you? Work only in your truth and integrity and you will become known as the "truthful animal *communicator". People will seek you out as they will know that you are one whose line of channel is held only in the highest truth and light and you will only give messages if you feel them to be true and accurate. The white lions are saying that it is so very important that you commit to this as they need a true channel for their communications — they have chosen you and this is why they invited you into the Inner Circle. This is a great privilege and you need to fully understand it. They chose you — you didn't choose them. Do you understand the significance of this message, dear one? Mandla sends his love to you, with thanks and gratitude for your commitment in helping his pride and being the human voice for many other animals on the planet at this time. There is an opportunity for you to co-write a book with Linda about your communications with Mandla, when the time is right but only after his custodian Linda allows for this and informs you it is time. This book has the great potential to touch the hearts and minds of many, for it is through animals that the love energy can be entrenched and activated in humans. Proceeds of this book can be donated to the Global White Lions Trust. If this is done with true honesty and integrity, Mandla says that abundance will flow towards the region in unimaginable waves and can benefit all.*

I was completely stunned by the message The true significance of my vision before I left for South Africa hit home as I realized the gravity of my commitment to my task. I felt very honoured, but very humble and hoped I could serve Mandla well. It gave me a lot to think about as I remembered the messages from the whales and the love they would spread throughout the oceans.

My hire car was returned and I was collected from Pooh Corner by a taxi to take me to the airport. My mind was full of images of whales, lions and unicorns and I found it difficult to engage in small talk with the driver as I contemplated the huge commitment that I had agreed to undertake. In the departure lounge, I sat and read some more words of wisdom from Credo Mutwa:

"We live in a strange world of separatism, a world in which things that really belong together and which ought to be seen as part of a great whole, are cruelly separated. Western man has come to believe that he is master of all living things, and that nature is there to be tamed at best, despised, broken and destroyed at worst. Until this attitude is erased from the human mind, westernized human beings will be a danger to all earthly life, including themselves."

I reflected on the severity of his profound message and its truth. I hoped that western man would start to wake up to the messages and wisdom of the animals.

As I sat on the airport bus that was to take me to the plane on the final leg of my journey, I noticed a large moth against the inside of the window. I asked it if it had anything to say, and it reminded me of the grasshopper that was on the bonnet of the car as we had left the white lions. I thought about the message that the grasshopper had given me: "Great change is coming". It had bravely clung onto the car until I'd got the message. The moth also reminded me of a message that I had intuited for Sharon. I had been given a civet as a power animal for her. She had hoped for a slightly bigger cat, but the message had been 'from tiny acorns mighty oaks grow', meaning that all the work she was doing with her salt crystals was going to be very important and in some way would tie in with all our work with planetary healing. It was also the first creature that Mandla had killed when he was set free, and there had been some doubt as to whether he would survive in the wild. The moth said that Mandla was letting us know that he could cope with his release and that it was the start of something big. Linda had asked me the significance of Mandla's small kill as the civet was evidently an important symbolic creature. I thanked the moth for its insight and asked it if would like to be released from the bus, but it said no as it was the guardian of the bus and would be monitoring more people, whether they knew it or not! Once again I pondered on what great changes were coming and how it would affect me and the planet?

As I boarded the plane, everyone took their seats and in front of me was a young man who was reaching up to put his hand luggage in the overhead locker. Emblazoned on his sweat shirt was a British Lions water-ski team motif. I smiled to myself; the lions were not going to let me forget them!

Basking sharks and Cornish ley lines

Jackie announced that she intended running a trip in the UK to swim with basking sharks off the Cornish coast. I felt that I had travelled to various destinations around the world to experience fabulous encounters, thanks to Jackie, and that it would be lovely to experience the wonders awaiting in British waters. I was intrigued as to what their role might be, and how they might be connected with other shark species and consciousness, and also discover their message for planetary healing. I was aware of the energy lines coming from Cornwall featured in the wonderful book *The Sun and The Serpent* by Paul Broadhurst and Hamish Miller.

I rushed to complete all my tasks before I could escape for a few days in glorious Cornwall. I'd received an email from Alex who I'd been with in Mexico, who was at the hotel in Newquay. It contained an uninspiring photo he'd taken from his hotel room – Newquay was suffering thick fog and heavy rain. Luckily, it wasn't long before the rain stopped and the sun came out, and I had a beautiful evening drive down to Cornwall, drinking in the fabulous scenery of Dartmoor and Bodmin. The proprietors at the B & B could not have been nicer and were so accommodating with my wheat and dairy intolerances. It was great to meet up with old travel companions that I hadn't seen since India and the Andaman Islands. Alex and I went walking in Newquay to get our bearings. It was great seeing the harbour, knowing that the next morning we would be going there to catch our boat, 'The Atlantic Diver', for a day on the ocean in search of our fishy friends. Alex told me that unfortunately that day's trip hadn't been lucky enough to spot any sharks, but they'd had fun swimming with some playful seals, so we were all hopeful that the next day's trip would find the sharks that some of the group had come so far to see.

The next morning the weather was beautiful. After breakfast, we loaded the car up with all our photographic gear, and made our way to the harbour. Another English friend of mine, Teri, who I'd gone all the way to South Africa to meet initially, had arrived early that morning to join our group, and we boarded the boat in high anticipation. There was quite a swell, and some of us felt a little queasy. I was fine until I sampled some of the water on the boat, which tasted disgusting as they used purifying tablets. After a few mouthfuls, I had to concentrate hard on the horizon to relieve any feelings of nausea that were creeping in! We had a wonderful day, but still no sightings of the baskers. We returned to Newquay and were greeted by the cheeky Atlantic grey seal, nicknamed Medallion Man, as he had a necklace of circular spots in his fur. The great thing about the boat was that it had a hydraulic lift that lowered you into the water. This was a far cry from trying to slip gracefully into the water off the side of the boat, and losing all hope of any graceful re-entry, as you sprawled like a beached whale, waiting to be hauled back in! The Captain, Chris, was lovely and really cared about the Cornish wildlife. He and his wife Annabelle spent their spare time helping out at the seal sanctuary nearby. The water was freezing, even with a wetsuit on and once Medallion Man had realized that we didn't have any fish to feed him, he snorted out a jet of water from his wonderful nostrils, telling me "You're useless"! He dashed off, like a dark torpedo, through the water to waylay the next boat that was returning. He was such a character and I loved his whiskery face and shining eyes. We were lifted back into the boat, only to have to climb up the harbour steps and monopolize the ladies toilet as we tried to heave ourselves out of our sodden wetsuits. However, once in dry clothes, we felt suitably thawed and got our lift back to the B & B. We decided to take Urs, the Swiss guy that I'd met with the humpbacks (and whose whale photograph of Gina is featured on the cover), out for fish and chips, as he'd never had any. So we sampled the delights of a Newquay 'chippy', which I have to say, we all enjoyed.

When I got to bed, I decided to see if I could tune into the sharks, to see if they had any messages. I had sensed their presence, but I felt they were a long way down in the ocean beneath us. The skipper had said that the plankton seemed to be quite deep, so they were probably feeding around us, but we were not able to see them. I felt I connected with a juvenile male, who said I could call him Bert! The terrible oil spill in the Gulf of Mexico had occurred, and I was anxious to know if the sharks were aware of this. The message was all about 'going deep'; they told me they were the deep thinkers. When they filter the water for food, they also monitor its quality and the vibrations of the molecules that travel thousands of miles. They said they were not monitoring in a fear-based, negative way, just assimilating and correlating information and bouncing back vibrational information to the whale sharks, who will all be migrating through the gulf stream from June onwards. So the baskers gave me very clear pictures of their spotted cousins! It was all about going deep to find the bigger picture. He was suggesting that it was signalling a time when, as a global nation, mankind has the opportunity to stand up and be counted and work to right our wrong doings to the planet. There was such an outcry about the mismanagement of the oil spill and the potential devastation of sea life and coastal habitats, and I feared for all the creatures that would be decimated and the chemicals in the dispersants that were more toxic than the oil. I hoped that the baskers could send messages of warnings to their bigger cousins to protect them. Since returning from the trip, I had been working with people around the world, using positive visualization to try and counteract the awful situation.

We had one more chance of a day's searching, but still did not see any sharks, so we moved further down the coast to Penzance. There were some strange energies around the town, and we experienced several altercations between people emanating from houses around the B & B overnight. I felt that some people struggled with the energy of the huge ley line, which ran so near from St. Michael's Mount, just down the road at Marazion.

We had booked the early ferry to the Scilly Isles, and marched through the streets of Penzance to the harbour to catch 'The Scillonian'. The sea was flat calm and we jostled to find the best seats on deck to scan the sea for any sightings of the sharks. Typically ,as we were about 20 minutes out of Penzance, we spotted around seven large telltale fins gliding through the water. We were sad that we couldn't leap off the ferry to swim with them, but at least we knew they were in the area. We also spotted a large pod of spotted common dolphins, leaping and cavorting in the sea, and wondered why they couldn't have shown themselves when we'd been on the boat!

As we arrived at St. Mary's, I felt it was a personal pilgrimage for my mother, as it had been a wish of hers to visit the Scilly Isles, and she had not been well enough in the end to make the journey, so I hoped she might enjoy it through my eyes. I was sure I could feel her presence as we disembarked, and I said that I hoped she would enjoy 'our' visit. We arranged to go on a seal and puffin wildlife boat trip out to the Bishop Rock lighthouse, and then onto the island of St Agnes. Rather like at Hermanus, the seals diced with death as the huge waves crashed onto the rocks around them. They appeared to be so totally at home in the frothing maelstrom of water. We spotted some puffins with beaks crammed with sand eels. As the sea was fairly calm, our little boat took us out to the lighthouse, which is the tallest in Britain and constantly pounded by the full force of the Atlantic. Looking out to sea, knowing the next land mass is America, was quite awe-inspiring.

When we arrived at St. Agnes, the weather started to deteriorate, but nothing could dampen our joy at seeing the beautiful flowers on this tiny island. We found a small stone labyrinth which had a wonderful energy and the rock formations were incredible. I walked around the labyrinth, noticing the effect on my breathing, as it was very calming.

On the ferry trip home, we saw the baskers in the same spot, feeding on the plankton-rich area just off Penzance, so we were hopeful that we would find them on our final boat trip the next morning from Porthkerris. However, despite the best efforts of the captain and his trusty collie dog, who gazed out to sea for us, ears pricked, we still had no luck. Returning to the beach at Porthcurno later on in the afternoon, we discovered that while we were out in the boat a large basker had nearly swam ashore. The life guard said that he'd swum out to see it, much to our exasperation. We also heard from the Newquay captain that the day after we'd left, they'd encountered several sharks and a small pod of orca! So we left feeling very sad that we hadn't managed to swim with any sharks, but we knew that this can happen with wild creatures, and of course they were wild and free to choose to interact with us or not. Obviously it wasn't so bad for Teri and I, but the rest of the group had come so far, so were very disappointed. We all left, in the rain, for our various destinations. I had some clients to visit on the way back to Somerset, and so with big hugs, I said my farewells.

Another chance

Some other friends of mine, Roxanne and Iain, who hadn't managed to get the time off work for Jackie's trip, decided that they would travel down and stay at a campsite near Porthcurno. They asked if Teri and I would like to try again to find the sharks. We jumped at the chance as it was such a beautiful area and we really hoped that at last we might meet the gentle giants. Our lovely friends had brought a barbeque and airbeds and all mod cons. I hadn't camped for years apart from the very posh tents we'd at Drakenstein with the lions, but that was in another league. It was such fun and the weather was glorious. We seemed fated again though, as the first time we went to Penzance to catch the boat trip the captain had cancelled it, and we stood on the harbour side, hearing the excited comments of the tourists from the previous trip relaying the sightings of sharks, porpoises etc. The captain promised us that he would arrange a trip for the next morning, a Sunday, so we hoped there would be enough numbers for us to go out. Luckily, another guy had driven all the way from Hungerford to swim with sharks, so we finally clambered into the small rib and made our way out to sea. It was another beautiful day, but again the sharks were eluding us. We chugged through the big waves around Lands End and were almost on the point of giving up and stopped to wait a little while around Sennen Cove, a favourite haunt for baskers. As if by magic, the water went calm, the sun shone down and suddenly we spotted a large dorsal fin cutting through the surface of the water – finally we had found a shark! We hurriedly fitted our masks, snorkels and fins and slid over the side of the boat into the chilly water. The shark was feeding right near us and we saw his gaping mouth and gills as he glided close by us. I could see his eye look at me and I knew it was Bert! He said he was happy to meet me in the physical, to which I answered "Not as glad as I am!" as he gracefully turned underneath me. He swam a little way off to collect more plankton and we had to hang on to the side of the boat to catch up with him. This was incredibly hard work, as we tried not to bump into each other and also avoid the propellers. Even the men were finding it challenging to hang on and I felt the muscles in my arms and shoulders complaining bitterly. However we got another chance to be with Bert as he kindly allowed us to swim right next to him. It was such a privilege. He asked me if I'd recorded and passed on his messages about the role of the basking sharks, and I said that I had. He said that I should be ready for more information from him when I wanted to connect with him in the future. I thanked him from the bottom of my heart for his help with monitoring the water. We then felt that we needed to leave him to his feeding, so we swam back to the boat, feeling triumphant at finally getting this wonderful encounter. I was so thrilled to actually meet the shark that I had communicated with a few weeks before. We shivered as the cold breeze chilled our soggy wetsuits, and we arrived back at the harbour feeling very cold. True to form, I managed to stand on a large rusty fish hook as we struggled to get our wetsuits off our quivering bodies. Luckily it hadn't penetrated over the barbs so I managed to pull it out, but it did bleed a bit.

The following day, we were lucky enough to get out in the boat again, though the weather had taken a turn for the worse. We were joined this time by some tourists who were hoping to see some marine life and learn more about the Cornish coast. We were all excited and headed towards Lands End and around the area we'd met Bert the day before, but the sea was quite rough, so we turned towards the other side of Penzance towards Porthkerris and found some ocean sunfish, who seemed to be waving at us with their fins as they floated like dinner plates on the surface of the water next to us. Eventually, we found two large baskers cruising through the water. To our amazement, one of them leapt forwards into the air and then in a sort of backwards flip. My friend Roxanne was ecstatic, as she had been communicating with a female shark who had called herself Lullie and she had said that she would show herself, like Bert did, but she obviously wanted to make sure that we would definitely feel her presence. She had guided Roxanne that there would be much more to see, and her display of acrobatics did not disappoint us. She was connecting Roxanne to all the shark life in Cornwall and rather like Bert, her male counterpart, was the female ambassador! I was so thrilled for her and honoured to witness Lullie's desire to connect with us. Sadly, Roxanne had suffered a broken back which had been operated on only fairly recently, and so when we swam with Bert, she struggled with the exertion and had to return to the boat prematurely. So meeting Lullie was a great treat for her. Unfortunately, we didn't have time to get in with the sharks to swim with them, but we were very content to enjoy the topside view! We also saw some porpoises leaping in the distance and some beautiful rare bird life in the cliff faces that towered above the sea.

When we returned to the campsite, a young woman who had been camped next to us was just cooking her tea. We'd previously exchanged pleasantries and she told us that she'd swum with a large pod of dolphins off the beach below us, much to our green-eyed disgust! We started to chat some more about what she did for a living and why she was there and it appeared that she had studied at Falmouth University doing wildlife conservation and told us what amazing field trips she'd had. She had even been to South Africa and met the penguin colony there. My ears pricked up and said that I'd met the penguins at Boulder Beach and were they the bird colony that she was talking about? She said yes. Her main interest however, was big cats, to which I replied that my main reason for going to South Africa was to meet the white lions. She asked where I'd been, as she was very well aware of the canned hunting industry and the way the main reason for the white lions bred in captivity was hidden from the tourists. When I said that Teri and I had been at Tsau her jaw dropped, as she said she'd spent a month with the royal pride collecting data for her thesis to gain her degree! I couldn't believe that the white lion's influence had followed us to a campsite in Cornwall and for all the tents, crammed into the campsite for the beautiful weekend, her's had to be the one right next to us! So we then had the most wonderful conversation about the messages of the white lions. I told her I felt they were driving me to spread their wisdom and that of the other amazing creatures, informing as many people as possible of the importance of the animal kingdom, for mankind and the healing of the planet. How wonderful that the lions could reach me in such an incredible way, to reinforce their influence on my life. More evidence of the wondrous ways the universe can work!

We were all sad to dismantle the tents the next morning. I knew I was going to miss the ocean view and the sight of the golden moon reflected in the sea. It had been quite noisy at the campsite and I'd found it hard to sleep. So I visualized going up the rays of the moon as I recalled its beauty, to meditate and ask for more information about my mission. It was a meditation I'd learnt many years before as a way to meet your guardian angel. I'd met some wonderful angelic beings before, but was a little surprised to meet a very feisty leprechaun who told me to get on with it and not delay in spreading the messages of the animals. He had a very stereotypical Irish accent that I tried not to laugh at! I remembered the leprechauns and divas in Tanis's book, and their messages that had started the whole process of my own book, and thanked my forthright messenger profusely. I was so grateful that we'd been so blessed with the whole experience and our glorious meetings with Bert and Lullie. I looked forwards to future communications with them.

Healing meditations from animals. Connecting with wild species

"Another world is not only possible, she is on her way.
On a quiet day, I can hear her breathing."
—Arundhati Roy

I am so blessed to have been able to travel on such a profound journey of reawakening, connecting with fabulous creatures all over the world. I thank them so much for all the wisdom that they have shared. I am so lucky to devote my life now to communicating with animals, and working to heal the challenges flagged up by them in order to help their human companions, both emotionally and physically. I am constantly amazed at the depth of knowledge and commitment they have, to bring us back on our path of enlightenment. The most amazing wisdom can be gained from a guinea pig to a whale, and my mission is to re-awaken that knowledge. Everyone of us can communicate with all living things and we all have the capacity to heal both ourselves and the planet. I hope to take groups of people to meet the lions and the whales in the future, so that they too can experience firsthand the energies and wisdom of these awesome beings. I now run courses and workshops to reawaken people's awareness of their healing skills and the following meditations form part of that reawakening. They are very powerful and should only be experienced in a safe quiet place, where you will not be disturbed.

Since starting the book, I have been guided to create a CD of meditations from the whales and the white lions, called *Whale Whispers, Lion Roars.* I was lucky enough to find just the right person to compose the music to deepen the experience of the meditations, no doubt sent to me by the universe and the animals! I also wanted to convey some of the meditations and visualizations to help connect with animals and

Our cheeky Atlantic grey seal, nicknamed 'Medallion Man'

ancient healing skills, which I use in my workshops. I feel that the most important message that the creatures of the planet want us to understand is that we have to be empowered. We have to reclaim our wisdom if we are going to make the changes necessary for the future of our planet, but first we have to make those changes within ourselves. The animals and cetaceans are giving us the tools to accomplish this. It's a good idea to record the meditations, as your own voice will have a very healing resonance for you and you will be able to relax more if you are guided on your journey, without trying to remember what comes next! Allow plenty of time for the various stages of the journeys to really experience the most from the meditation. Some soft background music also helps, but of course listening to the CD would really take you deeper! It's important to use the meditations as guidelines. If you feel that you need to create a different experience once you are meditating, follow your own guidance, allowing my words to fade into the background. Do what feels right for you! Your subconscious always gives you exactly what you need to learn the most from your meditations, and the creatures that you have asked to help you will always guide you, so that you can learn everything you need to know at this moment in time.

My rescue dog Winnie often co-facilitates my animal communication workshops and courses. She directs me telepathically as to what the group needs in order to further their skills. One particular instance was when I was driving down to Devon to an Equine Rehabilitation Sanctuary, where the course was to be held. Winnie piped up in my head and 'said' "they need to go into the heart of the Sphinx"! She had helped tremendously before, and I should by then have known to trust her judgement, but I felt that this might be a little advanced for the novice group, some of who were still quite conventional in their outlook and understanding of the connections between animals and their owners. So I wasn't sure how they would fare if I did as Winnie instructed. I needn't have worried, as Winnie gave me the whole meditation and everyone had the most incredible time. Winnie sat in the middle of the group with a very smug expression afterwards of "I told you so!" as everyone gave feedback of their experiences. The following meditation is what I channelled from Winnie.

Sphinx meditation
"The Heart of the Sphinx." Winnie's meditation!

Find yourself a quiet, comfortable place. Either sitting or lying down, focus on your breathing, feeling the gentle rise and fall of your abdomen as you breathe all the way in and all the way out. Being very gentle with yourself, with each out breath allow yourself to relax more and more, sinking into a soft, safe place of inner knowing. Each time you breathe out notice how beautifully your body responds, by relaxing more and more............... Feel yourself wrapped in light, feel the power of the light. See how light you are — weightless, see yourself start to float upwards in perfect safety and love. See yourself rise up above the mundane. Rise up above the ordinary basic human perceptions. Feel all the old

limitations and burdens of the old you falling away, until you see yourself as
pure light............. as a being of light. Allow yourself to be presented in front
of the awesome Sphinx in between the paws, at the Giza Plateau. Stand in
reverence of the beauty of this immense creation. Tune into the lion energy of this
sentient being, this iconic structure from eons into our past. Imagine that this huge
monument has a heart............. and you can hear and feel the heart and your
hearts can beat as one. Imagine that you can breathe as one with this lion being,
if it feels right. Imagine that you can enter the Sphinx, going beneath the great
lion's body, travelling through the underground catacombs, or travel through
time and space to discover more about your healing abilities. See yourself perhaps
in previous incarnations performing your healing skills, whatever feels right
for you............. When you feel ready find yourself once again in front of the
Sphinx and find a little piece of stone as a memento of your visit. Place it in your
pocket knowing that just by feeling the energy of the stone you can transport
yourself back to the Sphinx whenever you want, but just for now it is time to
return through time and space back into your chair. Notice how your body feels
now as changes and shifts in your consciousness have occurred at a cellular level.
Allow every cell in your body to remember who and what you were, and now
are again. Complete in the knowledge that you are a healer, you are a being of
light — you are a light worker! Rest now to assimilate all the changes.............
When you have absorbed all the information allow yourself to gently bring your
awareness back to the room, bringing back all your ancient wisdom.
When you are ready gently bring your awareness into a fully conscious
state, taking a deep breath, smiling and opening your eyes. Write down your
experiences and keep them as a record.

Power animal visualization

This is a lovely meditation to reconnect with nature and the qualities
and strengths of wild animals that we can connect with, as the Native
Americans believe embody all creatures.

Start by taking three deep breaths and as before allow each out breath to bring you into deeper and deeper relaxation. Rediscover that beautiful safe place within you............... that place that holds the key to your self love. Trust that you are the perfect being and that you are exactly where you need to be at this moment in time. There have been no mistakes, only learning experiences and opportunities to grow and develop into the wonderful person that you have always been! When you are ready imagine that you are standing at the bottom of a small hill. Feel yourself standing on the grass at the bottom of the hill. Feel the warm air on your face as the sun shines down on you, wrapping you in a golden glow. See yourself completely stripped of the day to day material trappings of your identity. See yourself completely bare, open to your divine core essence. See yourself shining there in all your glory, see how amazing you are! Now, when you are ready, ask to be met at the top of the hill by your power animal, whose strength will help you in your work. As you climb the hill............... there ahead of you is your animal friend who waits patiently for you to ascend. It greets you like a long lost friend, feel its soft fur or feathers caressing you. Allow this creature to take you on a journey to a special place to meet someone. This could be a wise person or healer, or maybe yourself as that wise person in a past life where you already performed this work. Let your animal take you now and go with whatever feels right for you............... When you come to your special place, notice all the details. When you meet your wise being ask all the questions you want, to get help for what you need to know at this moment in time...............
When you have finished your meeting with this healing person or being, thank them and allow the animal to take you back to the top of the hill...............
Once again, look for a memento of your journey and reconnection with your power animal. Know that you can hold this gift and connect with your animal any time you want, but for now it's time to leave. Extend your heart-felt gratitude and descend the hill, finding yourself at the bottom in the place where you started your journey. Rest awhile, absorbing all the experiences and knowledge that you have gained from your meetings, and then gently start to bring your awareness back to the room. Take a deep breath and open your eyes whenever you wish.

White lion 'lion heart' meditation
Finding your lion heart.

Take three deep breaths and on each out breath, give yourself permission to just 'let go' and notice how beautifully your body responds, as each time you breath out you feel yourself sinking deeper and deeper into that soft safe space, where you already know all the answers to all of your questions. Be aware of all the sounds outside the room and allow any sounds to just float in and out, helping you relax even more. Be aware of your breathing, feeling the gentle rise of your tummy as you breathe in and the gentle fall of your tummy as you breathe out, using the whole of your lungs, but being very gentle with yourself. Say to yourself, "each time I breathe out I can relax even more. Each time I breathe out I can relax even more", and notice how beautifully your body responds as each time you breathe out, you can notice how much more your body relaxes. Being aware of the floor beneath your feet, the clothes you're wearing and the chair you're sitting on, all keeping you very safe, warm and more and more relaxed............... When you are ready imagine that you are walking down a dusty track in Africa. As you look down at your bare feet you see the footprints you are leaving behind you as you take each step. You can feel the sun on your face and a gentle breeze in your hair. You know you are safe, protected and loved. Imagine you can call in the sacred white lion energy; know that with each step you take, you are closer to connecting with their strength and wisdom. You suddenly feel the urge to connect with the earth by walking on all fours and it feels wonderful to be so close to the earth energy. You feel changes in your body and to your amazement you realize that you are now walking on huge soft paws and you can see your paw prints in the soft ochre coloured earth. You feel the fluidity of your shoulders as you gracefully stride forwards, feeling the new strength in your limbs. Feel your beautiful tail behind you, balancing your movement, and a new sense of power within your heart............... Ahead of you is the great white lion, who has been waiting for you. Respectfully you greet him, as he introduces you to the rest of the pride. They rush to greet you like a long-lost relative and there is much roaring, rough and tumble, and rubbing of cheeks. Every lion is pleased to see you, and you are welcomed as an equal. You have never felt so much love and a sense of belonging. You ask the pride how you can maintain this feeling of power and connection and await their answers with excitement.

Spend time connecting with the pride and know that, from now on, you are a part of that pride, take time to really feel all the textures and the energies of the lions...............
You drink from a sacred watering hole, feeling the coolness of the water from this place of enlightenment soothe your being. You amaze yourself as you lap the sparkling water with your pride companions...............
When you have learnt all that you can for today, thank the pride for their help and love, and know that you can revisit them at any time you wish to get more information, but just for now it is time to come back, bringing your lion heart that still beats in your chest, and all the strength and wisdom you have gained. Find yourself walking back to the place on the track where you started your journey as you gradually regain your human form and your footprints retrace the human steps you made at the start of your journey. When you find yourself back at the start of your journey, just rest a while, allowing all the information and strength assimilate into every cell of your body. Feel your strong, compassionate, loving heart expand in your chest and feel that glow spread throughout your body. When you have assimilated and absorbed all you need to know today, gently bring yourself back, taking a deep breath, wiggling your fingers and toes and smiling, opening your eyes whenever you are ready, bringing yourself back to the room.

This is a great meditation to do with others, as the entire group becomes part of the pride. Notice who felt they were a lion or a lioness. On a recent course in France, we were working with a very timid cat. We all visualized shape-shifting into our lion forms and we took the cat with us. She also became a huge lioness and integrated with the pride. We all witnessed her grow in strength and confidence. When we brought her back in our meditation, the cat, who had been sleeping, got up, stretched, and sauntered out of the room as though she owned the place! The feedback from her owners, was that she was a different character – so self-possessed and unafraid. She really seemed to have found her lion heart! You can create this sense of strength and confidence with the help of the lions if you visualize taking them into the pride with you.

The whale Merkabah and the Rainbow Peace Walk

This beautiful meditation can aid planetary healing and participants often witness real change in their perception of the planet. The whales guide us in facilitating the best possible healing experience, and empower us to realize that we can create change. We can use the power of our minds in prayer to bring healing to the planet. It combines two meditations that I have been given by the whales and by a beautiful angel that channelled the 'peace walk' one morning as I lay in my bed. The whales guided me to combine the two meditations to create the most powerful planetary healing experience. This is another track on the CD which, when we recorded the music, found it to be a very profound experience.

Following the same relaxation process of focusing on your breath, give yourself permission to just 'be'. Knowing that you are perfect just as you are, and are exactly where you need to be at this moment in time. You have all the tools within you to create balance and harmony within yourself and your reality and that of the planet. So when you are ready, imagine that you are standing on a beautiful crystal pillar of light, in the middle of the ocean. It is very calm and you feel very safe and utterly loved and protected by the beautiful whales that come to surround you with their love and guidance. You can hear their vibrations through the water, filling your body as they help you in your healing work. They fill you with so much love and as you stand there you begin to feel the presence of an inverted pyramid beneath you as the pillar transforms into a beautiful pyramid with its point facing downwards. You are then suspended in light as another pyramid descends around you. This time it is an upright pyramid, creating the sacred geometric shape of the Merkabah, a beautiful star. You are held within the star which then becomes the centre of many larger stars that gently form around you. The whales ask you to imagine planet earth before you and to notice the areas that need help. Perhaps you might notice deforestation of the rainforests, or a darkness spreading in the ocean. Visualize whatever feels right and ask to be helped in healing these visions of the planet. Imagine a beautiful rainbow wrapping itself around the planet and then walk into the gorgeous colours...............

Step into the beautiful red. This is the red energy of hope. As you feel its vibration, imagine sending that red energy to all the parts of the world where there is despair, despondency, apathy and hopelessness, so that they may be transformed with the red energy of hope...............

Then step into the orange, a glowing pulsating orange that combines creative youth with ancient wisdom. Allow the orange to permeate all the world's minds to create positive healing solutions to all the seemingly unsolvable problems, bringing compromise, reason, and understanding of a bigger picture where all is one...............

Continue into the yellow, the yellow of intellect to further that understanding. Energize all the people who feel hatred and anger which stems from fear, fear that is held within us. Allow the yellow to gently soothe and calm that fear where it is stored in our bodies...............

Now enter the green which is the colour of pure love, harmony and balance. Imagine sending that green into the cell of every living thing to spread the word that the only true power is the power of love...............

Now walk through the blue and imagine all the oceans, seas, lakes, rivers and streams flowing into their banks and shores, spreading the blue of communication and healing into the countries and islands where the water meets land...............
Then step into the indigo of insight, intuition and knowledge of the higher self and send this in a prayer to the people of the world so they can find this insight...............

Finally walk into the violet of spiritual power and send it throughout the world for the highest good of all to bring peace and harmony to the earth *where there is still so much beauty.*

Now walk back until you reach the colour that you feel you need to heal yourself, for we can only heal others when we have healed ourselves, and we can only inspire peace in others when we have found peace in ourselves.

Spend time in your colour, letting its gentle vibration weave its magic on your being............... When you are ready, gently float back and look at the earth and see what has changed, Are the colours different? What has been absorbed? Watch now until every colour has been drawn into the earth to be absorbed and the healing can take place............... See what has changed, see the forests replenished and every leaf green and shining in the light. See all the creatures reclaiming their habitats. See the oceans full of life, every reef teeming with creatures and the coral full of energy and each microcosm of life thriving.

When you are ready, allow the Merkabah to dissolve and find yourself gently being guided back, standing on the shore, gazing out at the ocean.

The whales draw near to celebrate the healing that has taken place – you can hear their sound filling your body once more as they sing in salutation.

Give thanks for their help and the healing that has taken place.

Gently start to bring your awareness back to the room, bringing back all the love from the whales. Resting and absorbing all that you have experienced, until you are ready to open your eyes.

The definition of peace is:
"A condition in which there is no war, violence or disorder, but quietness and calm."

Roots in Atlantis

This is a beautiful meditation for reconnecting with your ancient healing skills in Atlantis. It also helps to connect you with what I call 'light crystal' energy, which I discovered when helping my mother with her cancer. I was guided to place etheric light crystal pillars within her body to help ease her pain. To my amazement and that of the medical team working with her, it seemed to work. This meditation can help you heal yourself and others using the Atlantean crystals. The light crystal energy can come in many forms, which I wrote about in my book, *An Exchange of Love*, but suffice to say that it is wonderful to be open to whatever way this energy may manifest. The dolphins taught me this meditation, and seem very ready and willing to help us reconnect with our Atlantean pasts, so this meditation is a lovely way of calling in their energy so they can help you. Obviously there have been less joyful times in Atlantis and I have experienced a regression where I was aware of the genetic engineering taking place. In that lifetime, I did nothing to stop it or help the mutated creatures, so I paid a heavy price. I feel this is why in my current incarnation, I need to constantly work for the very highest good of all the animal kingdom and be their voice to help the planet. This meditation can help you find your healing gifts from the golden age of Atlantis, so that you can put them to good use again!

Finding a quiet safe place, allow yourself to become comfortable in an easy chair, really feel your feet on the floor and acknowledge your deep connection to Mother Earth.............. Really get a sense of her beauty. Set your intention to reclaim your healing powers and to receive beautiful healing from the dolphins and the light crystals. So start by taking three lovely deep breaths, giving yourself permission on each out breath to let go more and more. Imagine the beautiful healing energy of the dolphins drawing close to you. Imagine their sound filling your body. Feel them wrapping you in white light and a great sense of peace permeating your being. If you have any fear of water, allow the dolphins to help you feel completely safe and protected and very much loved. When you are ready, focus your attention on the soles of your feet.............. Imagine they can open up and you can grow the most beautiful roots down into the ground. Imagine them going deeper and deeper.............. Travel through all the rocks and crystalline structures, the metals, deeper and deeper back through time and space. Allow them to finally arrive in a fabulous lake, feel the coolness as your roots enter the water. It is the most beautiful blue. Imagine that you can drink up the water with your roots which then pours into your body. This may be a blue energy or maybe a beautiful blue/gold, go with whatever feels right for you. Feel the energy of the water entering your body............... Knowing that you are very safe, allow your core essence to journey down now through your roots, as the lovely water energy carries you back down to the lake.............. When you arrive you feel the presence of many beings welcoming you. Notice how they look. These are ancient Atlantean beings and they are so happy that the dolphins have brought you home. The dolphins arrive in the lake and guide you down under the water as they lead you through a short tunnel filled with light. When they lead you through, you come out onto the shore of the most incredible landscape.............. You sense the most wonderful crystal temples. Notice what else is around you and how familiar it might be as you start to remember when you spent lifetimes here. Be guided to enter one of the temples, and before you there is a huge bed made of crystal, which seems like clear quartz, but has an inner fire of light that shines out. Lie on the bed and allow the light from the crystals to send healing light through your whole body. Clearing any energy blocks on an emotional or physical level................, feel your whole body being cleansed.............. When you are ready, imagine entering an amphitheatre, which at first seems to be made of stone. You sit in on a kind of throne and as you close your eyes and concentrate, the whole place becomes filled with light crystal energy. See any people or animals that you wish to give healing to, sitting or lying, on the crystal floor. See them filled with light. Perhaps, see yourself working with them as you once did in that ancient time, ask to be shown how you once used your healing skills.............. Some of these dear souls may have passed over, but they have needed healing to help them on their way, so imagine them filled with light and then soaring upwards, so that they can connect with their future lifetimes, or healing work in spirit.............. Find a small token of the Atlantean energy, maybe a small crystal, to bring home with you, so that you can reconnect with the light crystal energy whenever you wish. Know you can journey here at any time to bring healing to yourself and others, but just for now, it's time for you to travel back with the dolphins, making your way back through the tunnel, back to the lake.............. Thank the ancient beings, and the dolphins, for welcoming you home and for allowing all the healing to take *place, and reminding you of your ancient heritage and skills. You know you can return whenever you wish, but just for now it's time to journey back up through your roots, allowing the beautiful water energy to carry you back up. The colour may be the same, or it may have changed, just notice how it makes you feel, as you journey back up into your body, once again taking on your human form............. Allow yourself to rest and absorb your experiences, notice how your body feels. When you are ready, allow yourself to return to the room, take a deep breath, bringing back all the healing and re-awakened skills.*

Meeting your ancient self

This is another lovely meditation, where you can connect with your ancient shamanic, tribal past. It's a good idea to play some soft drumming music to help carry you on your journey of rediscovery about your past. Many indigenous tribes still have their healers or Shamans, who connect with Mother Earth and the animals to perform their healing skills. I rescued a horse who I know has been my medicine horse in a lifetime when I was a Northern Cree Indian in North America. He helps me in my sessions working with people and their horses. He is a very powerful being and has to be treated as an equal and I know we have had many lifetimes together. He is helping me send healing to the wild mustangs, who are suffering at the hands of humans. They are part of the heritage that is being destroyed to make way for mining, pipelines and cattle. They are as sacred as the wild horses that I met in South Africa and it is so important to remain in the wild, working with Mother Earth. The horses I have worked with have taught me all about my Shamanic heritage, allowing me to work with skills that I once would have used in my ancient tribal past life. I am so grateful to them, as they have allowed me to work with dimensions and concepts that were long lost in my memory and they gave me this meditation to help others rediscover their own tools.

*So, whenever you are ready, take gentle deep breaths, feeling the rise of your abdomen as you breathe all the way in, and the gentle fall as you breathe all the way out............... Notice how beautifully your body responds, as each time you breathe out you give yourself permission to just let go............... Feel yourself sinking deeper and deeper into a wonderful place of knowing as you release any residual tension from your body, breathing it out. Imagine breathing in peace and breathing out tension, breathing in love and breathing out fear. Allow all the sounds outside the room to just float in and float out............... You can deal with any thoughts that clutter your mind later. Just follow your breath and allow the sound of the music and your breathing to help you relax more and more. This is a journey of rediscovery and a reclaiming of ancient healing powers that you once had. Now is the time to remember these skills. Now is the time to work with the animals and Mother Nature. So whenever you are ready, imagine that you are walking along a track. You feel a gentle breeze in your hair and the warmth of the sun on your face. You can hear the birds and insects all around you. You feel a great sense of anticipation, as you know you are journeying to meet your ancient self and your tribal people. Ahead of you in the distance is a huge rock face and you can see that it has many caves. Allow yourself to walk towards the caves and be guided as to which one you feel most drawn to enter...............
As you go inside, notice who or what is waiting to welcome you there. They will lead you into your past and show you how you once healed people and animals. Be open to meeting whoever presents themselves. You may see yourself dressed as you would have been in that past life and performing your healing skills. Ask what your name was and what other tribe's people are called. See your home and where and how you once lived. Meet with a tribal elder and ask whatever questions you need answering to help you on your healing path. Let them help you now..............., knowing you can return whenever you wish, but just for now it's time to bring yourself back into the present time. Ask to be given a gift from the earth to bring back with you, to remind you of your skills and to tune into your tribe at any time............... Giving thanks and saying farewell, leave your tribe now and make your way through the cave and back out into the sunlight once more, bringing back all that knowledge with you...............*

The great white lion comes to greet you!

Find yourself walking back up the path and rest at the place where you started your journey. Assimilating all the information you have re-learnt and remembered. When you are ready, take a deep breath, taking your time and opening your eyes as soon as you are able.

Meeting the keeper of your crystal

This is another lovely meditation to connect with the crystal beings of the planet. You may be drawn to work with physical crystals as well as the etheric. With this journey you can ask to experience the healing properties of any crystal, perhaps asking which crystal you most need to connect with at this moment in time. Perhaps you need protection or grounding or more help with intuitive powers. Crystals have amazing properties and can be programmed to work in whatever way is most appropriate both for you or the people you are wishing to help.

Many animals I work with suggest which crystal they would like and which would most benefit their human companion or their environment. A beautiful white lion, who was bred in captivity and sent to a zoo, asked me to send rose quartz crystal energy into his cage and enclosure to help him cope with his incarceration. I was horrified to learn that he was related to the magnificent white lion who I met in the wild at Tsau. That such a beast should be contained in that situation was hard to bear, but perhaps his role is like the captive dolphins that I met in the Dominican Republic: to affect and raise the consciousness of the unsuspecting visitors to the zoo. I hoped my efforts to send him the rose quartz energy would help. I remembered the same energy around the baby whale that I swam with, and called in that beautiful quality of love and protection for the lion. I have also loved placing etheric crystals in wonderful places around the world, especially the beautiful orb that the pilot whale took from me when I was in the Azores. This is a meditation that can help you tune into the crystalline structures of the planet and remember how to use crystals in whatever way is right for you.

Once again, take time to fully relax your body, being very gentle with yourself. Know that you are safe and very much loved. Focusing on your breath, gradually allow yourself to release more and more, allowing all tension to drain from your being. Ask to be shown how you can work with crystals and that you may learn whatever you need to know at this moment in time. When you are ready, imagine that your feet can open up and you can grow wonderful roots down into the earth – down through the floor, down and down and down, deeper and deeper, until they find themselves wrapping around a beautiful crystal. Notice if it seems smooth or rough? What colour is it? How does it make you feel?.............. Imagine that you can travel down your roots and step inside the crystal, passing inside, in whatever way feels right to you. There you will meet the keeper or guardian, in whatever form this might take. Know that you can ask questions from the guardian. Ask now and be shown what you need to remember.............. You will feel yourself filled with the beautiful healing energy of the crystal, see how you can use that energy to most benefit yourself and others. Ask for any further advice that can be given to you today, to aid your healing soul journey.............. When you are ready, thank the guardian for their advice, and be given a small fragment of the crystal as a keepsake and reminder of what you have learnt, so that you can link in with that wisdom whenever you wish.............. Now it is time to journey back, feel yourself withdrawing from the crystal and journeying back up your roots, up and up until you feel yourself coming back into your body, bringing back all the crystal wisdom and your small piece that reconnects you at any time. Taking your time, gently bring your awareness and crystal wisdom back.............. Back into your waking consciousness, take a deep breath and open your eyes whenever you are ready.

The room of the moon and the sun

This beautiful meditation was first given to me by a wonderful catalyst in my life, Thea Holly. She was the first person who facilitated my connection with outer planetary and inner earth beings. I have since adapted the meditation to suit my animal communication workshops, but everyone who has tried it has found wonderful gifts in the 'rooms'. My first journey into the room of the sun taught me that I would always have a never- ending supply of light crystals to work with. I 'saw' a mountain of crystals that never seemed to diminish, however many I took to work with. This reinforced my awareness that we are always guided and given exactly the right tools to work with when we need them. Other group participants have returned from the meditation, having been given a lit candle to symbolize that they will always be guided by the light. It's always a very empowering experience and lovely to have the male and female balance of the sun and the moon. The addition of mirrors in the room also gives you an idea of your past, present, and future roles and you can get a clear indication of just how much you have progressed on your soul journey. So see if this meditation resonates with you and I hope you gain as much from it as I did!

Finding a comfy chair, allow yourself to sink further and further into your quiet inner space. Focus on your breath, being very gentle with yourself. Feel yourself wrapped in light, keeping you very safe and protected. With each out breath, feel yourself relaxing more and more, going deeper into your inner knowing. Let all external sounds float in and out of your mind and bring your attention back to your breath. Become aware of the sound of your breath and the beautiful way it releases all remaining tension from your body............... When you are ready, imagine you are sitting in a very beautiful chair. In front of you there is a strip of carpet that leads away from you up two steps that lead into a long corridor. Imagine that you can stand up and walk along the carpet, climbing the steps and finding yourself walking along the corridor. You are searching for the door that leads into the room of the sun, and you soon find a door that has the symbol of the sun written or painted on it. Study the door, intuiting all the details............... Is it old or new? Is it made of wood or metal? What is the handle like? Get a real sense of all the details............... When you are ready, turn or push the handle and enter the room. It will be filled with sunlight. Again, notice what is contained in the room. There will be a guardian of the room waiting to help you and to show you how far you have come on your healing journey. Meet the guardian now and be open to whoever or whatever they might be. They will show you three mirrors which symbolize your past, present and future. You may see yourself in a past life or just as a child in this life............... Just go with whatever feels right for you, knowing that you will learn much about where you have come from, which makes you the wonderful person you are today. Ask to be shown what your future role will be as a healer and light worker. If this is a little challenging, just ask for help from your animal friends, and they will guide you to the best possible understanding. You may also ask any questions or advice in order to further your awakening and awareness. So look now and see what you can learn............... When you are ready, thank the guardian for all their help and ask to be given a gift as a symbol of the wisdom of the room. This gift is the manifestation of your healing skills and by connecting with it at any time in the future you will reconnect and re-empower that inner knowing............... So, having shown your gratitude, make your way back to

*the door and step back through into the corridor, closing the door gently behind
you. Walk along the corridor a little further, until you find the door that leads
into the room of the moon. Again, notice the details of the door — its condition,
colour and type............... You open the door and step into the most beautiful
moonlight that wraps you in love. Notice what else is in the room, intuiting its
contents. Again ask to meet the guardian of the room who will give you yet more
advice. Notice how each room makes you feel. Ask to be shown whatever you
need, to compliment what you learnt in the room of the sun. Explore the room and
ask your questions, so that you can absorb as much information as possible. See
how the moon energy affects you. Explore it now............... When you feel you
have gleaned as much information as you can for today, thank the guardian and
the room for all their wisdom. Again, bring a gift from the room to allow you to
connect with its energy whenever you wish. You may understand the meaning
of the gift immediately or its significance may take a few days to become clear,
but just know that the understanding will come. Step through the door, closing it
behind you and turn to walk back down the corridor, along the carpet, down the
two steps and sitting back once more in your beautiful chair...............
Rest awhile, absorbing all the information you've been given.
When you have absorbed and assimilated all that you have learnt, gently
start to bring your awareness back to the room. Take a deep breath and
open your eyes whenever you are ready.*

The key to your heart

This is a meditation that incorporates the experience I had in the beautiful
temple of Hathor at Deir El Medina. You too can reach through the wall
and reclaim the key to your heart and reconnect with your star-being
family, being reminded of new or long forgotten ways to heal yourself and
others. I use this meditation in my 'gateways to the ancients' workshop
and it always results in the most incredible feedback from course
participants. It is a very powerful experiential meditation.

Find yourself a comfortable place to lie, where your back and head is well supported, so that you can really relax and release all tension from your body. Take some deep breaths and allow your whole body to let go. Feel each group of muscles working up from your feet, becoming more and more relaxed. Breathing in peace and breathing out tension, and notice how your body responds as it relaxes more and more. Feel yourself bathed in light, knowing you are very safe and very much loved. Whenever you are ready, imagine you can walk through the light and find yourself on a ancient stone path. You feel the heat of the Egyptian sun on your face as you walk through the thin veil that leads you back in time. You find yourself entering a beautiful temple dedicated to Hathor the goddess of healing and joy. You see the brightly coloured reliefs on the pillars and walls, as though freshly painted. See the wonderful face of the goddess and her lovely cows ears, smiling down at you. You enter the temple and find the small inner sanctum............... You notice the hieroglyphs on the walls, displaying their ancient messages. Suddenly, as you study the wall, the images start to move, as the wall seems to shimmer. You feel drawn to reach into the wall with your arm. You seem to pass through layers effortlessly. Your hand reaches and eventually finds a beautiful key. Bring back the key and place it in your heart............... Notice how this makes you feel. You then feel as though an opening appears in the top of your head and ancient codes seem to be dropped deep inside of your being. You might not understand what these codes mean, but know that all will be unveiled in divine and perfect order. These will give you a deeper awareness of the divine purpose of your uniqueness............... When you feel that you have received all your codes, allow the opening to gently close, sealing in all the wisdom that has been downloaded into you. You notice above you an opening in the ceiling of the sanctum, that you hadn't been aware of before and you feel the presence of some very special beings who are waiting to communicate with you. You might imagine a ring of lights above you that seem to draw you upwards. You can surrender to the process of joining them, or you may feel that you would prefer to remain in the temple, to process your experience. Do whatever feels right for you............... These beings wish to reconnect you with your star being heritage and show you new ways of healing and perhaps their vision of how to *help the Earth. For whatever befalls the Earth affects all the other planets, which is why these beings want to help us. Should you wish to join them, you may meet a council of different beings, who wish to share their insights with you. Connect with them with the deepest respect, and accept their wisdom with gratitude. You may learn that you once took their form in past incarnations, and you feel the depth of their love for your willingness to be of service and the challenges of your human form. Be open to learning from them now............... Bring back their wisdom and messages of hope and ask for ways to reconnect with them whenever it is appropriate. Perhaps there is an animal in your life that connects with these beings and can help you gain yet more wisdom from them. Just ask to be shown how............... Thank the beings for all their help and wisdom. You will be gently lowered back into the temple room. You see that the once fluid wall appears solid, but you know you can feel a change in your heart where your ancient key of wisdom now resides. You feel a huge sense of expansion within your being, as you make your way out of the temple, giving thanks to Hathor for protecting you and allowing you to acquire so much information within her beautiful temple, for she wishes you nothing but healing and joy. Make your way back up the ancient path; everything seems so bright back out in the sunshine. You walk back through the veil of time, back into the here and now. When you find yourself at the place where you started your journey, rest awhile, assimilating all your experiences and allowing the process of absorbing all the information to continue within your being............... Very gently start to bring your awareness back to the room, taking a deep breath, stretching your fingers and toes and opening your eyes whenever you are ready............... Write down all the information and details of your experiences. You may feel that you would like to draw or paint your key or the energy of the beings, which would help to anchor their presence and their information in your reality.*

It's always a good idea to record your meditations, by writing or drawing the details. You often find that you had forgotten key components of the journey when you re-read your findings, and you also discover how much has unfolded in your reality since your journey, as you now understand far more of what you were shown previously. My dog Winnie often connects with outer planetary beings and I can feel the change in her energy when she is working with them. Many horses work this way and of course most of the cetaceans seem to have a direct line to the Universe and the wondrous beings there! I truly hope that you find these meditations as powerful as I have, and that you gain the most wisdom and healing possible from them.

Speaking to dolphins – how to communicate with wild creatures

The following is an interview I gave to help people to connect with wild dolphins, either physically, if they were lucky enough to get the chance to swim with them, or remotely, knowing that we can all connect with any living thing if we open our hearts and minds.

What is the dolphins' role on earth, especially at this time of great change leading up to 2012?

I feel the dolphins' role is changing, from being a gentle saviour of seamen and playmate of snorkelers, to one of mirroring what man is doing to the planet. I feel their previous role was to bring joy and re-empowerment to us. But now I feel it is not what can they do for us, but what can we do to heal them? There has finally been such uproar and horror of the daily massacre of dolphins in Japan and the mercury poisoning of people eating dolphin meat. Wonderful documentaries with courageous film makers have highlighted the scale of the carnage that these beautiful creatures have endured to a deaf and blind world. At last their voice is being heard. I feel the dolphins are showing us that if we can do this to the dolphins and whales, it's a very sad world that we are living in. I feel the dolphins are reminding us of the fate of Atlantis and they are forcing us to sit up and take notice of the stupidity and short sightedness of what mankind is doing to the planet. I feel on some deep level the dolphin consciousness has agreed to this, so that we finally get the message because 2012 is the age of new awareness and we have to raise our vibration to bring about that change. I felt, after listening to the captive dolphins, that they had chosen that role in order to reach more humans, who would not otherwise interact with them. The tourists who brought their families to the oceanariums to watch the displays and swim with the dolphins were being affected on levels they were totally unaware of. The dolphin I encountered understood that captivity was a state of mind and she was able to journey astrally whenever she needed re-balancing. It seemed like a definite choice in her current incarnation. What courage and commitment to the planet, to choose such a life?

What kind of healing powers do the dolphins have and how do you believe they are able to heal like this?

I feel they have the ability to scan auras and chakras on a physical, mental, emotional and spiritual level. With their sonar they can check and rebalance our energy centres, which is why autistic children can become more empowered and start to speak after interacting with them.

How do dolphins communicate telepathically with us? How can we connect with them in this way? What does it feel like communicating with dolphins?

Being in the water with wild dolphins is almost indescribable. When you are lucky enough for a dolphin to freely choose to interact with you, you are truly blessed. I feel their energy is so pure that they can tune into us practically before we even get into the water and once near us they affect the water molecules in our bodies with their vibration. When you remember how much of our bodies are made up of water and the effect of positive energy on water molecules, you can see how amazing it must feel to be connected to them. It's about being open to listening to telepathic communication in your head and trusting your gut feelings that it is not just your imagination. These are multi-dimensional sentient beings that know and understand the fragility of the planet far better than we do.

Please give some tips for readers on how to connect with the dolphins, firstly if they are actually in the water with them, secondly, if they aren't even near the ocean but wish to connect with their energies.

You can connect with a dolphin physically just like any other creature, through a heart to heart connection. You imagine a cord or bridge of love connecting your hearts and send all the love you can along that cord or bridge, whilst imagining your heart centre opening like a beautiful flower with all its petals unfurling. This works equally well at a distance, either remembering a previous encounter or an imaginary one. Just open your hearts and listen. Dolphins enter our dream states, where they can access us more easily or pop into our meditations, where our mistrustful, logical minds can't interfere. If you are having any difficulty, a good question to ask yourself is "if this dolphin could speak what might it say"? Then write down whatever comes to mind. You may surprise yourself by the information that comes through. Ask the question "how can I help, what do I need to know at this time for the very highest good of all"?

Earth whispering

I have been guided now to start running courses that deepen our awareness of our abilities to connect with any living thing on our beautiful planet and the Earth itself. By lying on the ground and allowing yourself to surrender to the beauty of the planet, you can expand your awareness to communicate with Mother Earth. On a recent visit to France, where I was running an Animal Communication course, I was guided to take the group into a beautiful wood nearby. We all lay on the forest floor, and sent our love deep into the earth. While we were doing this, hordes of yellow butterflies surrounded us. They seemed to come from nowhere. It was the most wonderful sight. We sent out so much love to the planet and the universe and it was as though the butterflies were celebrating this and enjoying the love! Just as suddenly they disappeared, but left the message that we need to remember to connect with everything, even the insects, as they too have a voice. I remembered the wisdom I'd been given by a common housefly on several occasions and the cockroach in Mexico with very strong opinions! I feel it is imperative that we rediscover our connection to Earth, by really listening to her and all her inhabitants in nature. We have become materialistic and conditioned to take and not give. The time has come to repay our debt and give back to the Earth, with the help of the animals who wish to guide us back. I hope to run courses with the help of the white lions and the whales in the near future and perhaps when you read this book you may feel drawn to join me.

Messages from trees, rocks and water spirits

The following accounts are what I scribbled down when connecting to these spirits. There is also a communication with a huge Siriun being who had a lot to say about my current status. They were intuited in 2004 just after my mother's passing and my separation from my husband. Even now, when I re-read them, I learn more understanding from their words and the importance of my role to help and play a part of the re-awakening of so many of us who are still asleep. So many people are blind to the importance of the animal kingdom, and the necessity to start listening to planet's needs instead of their own. There is no doubt great change is coming and it is up to us to make sure that these changes are positive and that we learn from our mistakes.

The ancient fir

"I speak with an ancient tongue, long forgotten. No one 'speaks' anymore,
neither do they listen. I am sad for the air I breathe and the water I drink.
It is not whole, it is dark and devoid of life and light force. Thank you for your
healing tears and the gold of your love, which reached the very core of my being.
Thank you for your sweet music that recalled and returned our spirits.
They are laughing and chattering once more and it makes me want to shout
out loud. Beware, listen to the mother, and take heed. Guard the guardians.
Show then your open honest truth in your hearts, for the earth is a fragile
being and is desperate for your love."

I remember the tears that poured from my eyes as we sang and chanted around this immense tree. I was guided to place my hands on its mighty trunk and I felt a gold energy pouring from my hands into the tree. I could feel that its spirit was being lifted as though it had been ignored for so long and felt a gratitude towards us for learning to listen to its wisdom. I felt that it was the energy of this tree that might have inspired Tolkien to create the Ents in his famous books.

Message from a stone

This small boulder was in the middle of a stream that trickled past me. I sat on its bank with paper and pen and just wrote whatever came into my mind. This is what it told me in the midst of my emotional turmoil:

"I am symbolic of where you are in your life — a big block in a stream of
emotions and thought patterns. Think of me and the present events as a
huge stepping stone, to leap forward, onwards and upwards. There is nothing
to hold you back, only your fear and that is just a thought which can be
changed. Take heart, have faith, this is just the beginning. Use my solidity
as a strong platform, a launching pad, and take flight!"

I'm still stunned by the profundity of its words and its relevance to so many of us caught in patterns of self-doubt and limitation. How amazing that, if we just take the time, we can learn so much about ourselves and what we need to heal, just by tuning in to nature.

The next piece of good advice came from a water diva who said its name was 'Lactern'. I pondered on the resemblance to the word lectern, which is the stand for a bible or used by a 'lecturer'! They were very strong words to motivate me!

"Do you wish to become large and grow strong in the light? Or do you wish to remain small and hidden in the dark? Break out and stand tall in your conviction. Sharpen the claws of your wit, polish the shield of your defences, to enlighten and bring light to those who are lost in grief. Grieving for the loss of light and the clarity it brings as they struggle and stumble onward. Take their hands and guide them to the light and everlasting love."

These words still move me today. As I share them with you I realize their relevance to so many of us committed to work with the light and the challenges this can bring. It was certainly a very challenging time for me as I felt so much of the 'old' me being stripped away. The following dialogue that I wrote down from my interaction with a very large being makes even more sense to me now as I relay it in 2010.

"You are being re-aligned. Soon your whole being will be unrecognisable to your previous self. You are metamorphosizing at a cellular level. This is why you feel restless at night and confused about yourself by day. As you know, you can no longer eat the same foods or dietary regime. This is because you are changing so fundamentally, so that the previous Madeleine will no longer exist. Your past relationships and personal connections will find it difficult to recognize you as they expect to find or feel the 'old' you and that 'you' is nowhere to be found. Your new persona is being created so that you can take up the work and duties being prepared for you. Have no fear. All is as it

should be and your path will soon become clear. I am from Sirius and we are
collating data and information regarding light workers and co-workers.
We need to know their progress so that planetary healing can be initiated.
All is adjustment and fine tuning and is on course for your greater
awareness and understanding. This will come to pass. There are also
light beings from Chiron, who are helping this ailing planet.
Activate the light grids to regenerate, recharge and renew!"

So much becomes clearer now as I see how I was being prepared to undertake my mission, the mission that has become even more evident since connecting with the whales and more recently with the white lions. I think many of us are struggling with our diets with allergies and intolerances to wheat and dairy because of the chemicals used in modern farming. I feel the more sensitive we are to our environment, the more sensitive we are to what we put into our bodies. I have felt for a long while that eating meat was wrong. I remember having to cook meat for my husband and feeling the stress in the meat from the slaughtered animals. It was awful, and maybe yet another reason why we're not together anymore!

It has been quite a journey and a privilege to share it with you. I hope that it inspires you to listen to the power and wisdom of the animals, for they are truly our greatest teachers and we have so much to learn! I hope to share a few more journeys with people who feel drawn to learn from the wild creatures. So in the future, I will accompany like-minded souls to meet the white lions in South Africa and I plan to take groups to meet the whales. I have been guided by the lions to create a course that facilitates deep awareness of 'earth whispering', so that more people can really learn to listen to the planet. I also want others to share in the physical connection and healing which can take place in close proximity of these awesome beings. I know that I have to balance my impact on the environment with air travel, and there will come a time soon when I will have to set my roots down in the place where I am needed most so that I may continue my tasks. The beauty of 'whispering' is that you can 'hear' what the animals are saying wherever you are – you just have to open your heart!

> *"In the beginning of all things, wisdom and knowledge were with*
> *the animals, for Tirawa, the One Above, did not speak directly to man.*
> *He sent certain animals to tell men that he showed himself through*
> *the beast and that from them, and from the stars and the sun and*
> *moon should man learn… all things tell of Tirawa."*
> —Eagle Chief (Letakos-Lesa) Pawnee

Final message from the humpbacks

"We beseech you to remember our messages of love that we spread through the oceans. Please help us by singing our song of love. Fear and negativity destroys the heart of the planet quicker than any pollutant – in fact it is an emotional pollutant that we struggle to overcome. So join us with the vibration of love and peace that you can sing out in harmony with us. This is our greatest, most powerful strategy, but we need your help. As you raise the vibration of positive energy, you work with us to raise the vibration of the whole. We connect with the whole whale collective, where every cetacean species holds that message of love for the planet. Blessings and peace from the Whale Consciousness."

Dr. Masaru Emoto on healing the gulf

Let us thank Dr. Emoto for this prayer of Ho'oponopono. Please share this with your friends and contacts around the world. He sends this prayer, "*With Our Love*". To speak it with sincerity is powerful and humbling:

Now let's give energy of love and gratitude to the waters and all the living creatures in Mexico Gulf by praying like this:

To the water, whales, dolphins, pelicans, fishes, shellfishes,
planktons, corals, algae and all creatures in our Gulf of Mexico
I apologize.
Please forgive me.
Thank you.
I love you.

—Masaru Emoto

May 9th 2010

ACKNOWLEDGEMENTS

Huge thanks to Sabine and everyone at Findhorn Press for accepting this book and having faith in my work. It's been quite a journey, conveying the creature's messages in the wild to the pages here. So I'm so grateful to have the opportunity to pass the messages on, and be the conduit for all the beings who have had the patience and willingness to share their wisdom with me. I'd like to thank all the incredible creatures, especially Gina and her baby, Mandla, Marah, Nebu and all the white lions, Sonny the whale shark, Rajan, and Bubbly the Indian elephant. Also Bert the basking shark, and Pillow, Teazle and Winnie – very special dogs in my life.

To all my family and my children for their patience, especially Cameron, as we've fought over who was going to use the computer! I'd also like to thank Jenny Smedley for all her help and encouragement in making me believe that I could write and for just 'being there'. Big hug to Eric Ehrke, for giving me permission to share his channelling from our encounters, and all the wonderful messages he conveys from the cetaceans.

Thanks to Urs Buehler, Karen-Jane Dudley, Jason Turner, Alexander Turoff, and James Edwards, for allowing me to use their photographs of our trips. Thanks also to Jacqueline Russell for her photograph of Rajan and for creating all the wonderful journeys with 'Wild Ocean Adventures', and to Linda Tucker for taking the time to write the foreword and for the excellent work she does for the sacred white lions. Love to Cordelia Brabbs for her literary guidance. Big thanks to Joan for holding the fort while I'm away on my travels and to Thea Holly for being the catalyst and beautiful person that she is. I'd also like to thank Jerome O'Connell for his incredible talent, collaborating on the *Whale Whispers* CD, which features the energy and meditations of some of the creatures in the book. We had such an emotional time recording it, with all the awesome beings that joined us in the studio, especially the ancient whale being, Nagwal, who helped us create the track called 'The Lagoon of Nagwal' on the CD. Jerome's channelled whale sound from Nagwal on the cello reduced us both to tears. Look out for it on the CD! I really hope that everyone enjoys the meditations as much as we did creating them.

Finally of course, huge thanks to my mum!

RESOURCES

Whale Whispers, Lion Roars, CD by Madeleine Walker, published by Findhorn Press.

http://ericehrke.wordpress.com
Reflections of Ourselves. Beautiful messages in blogs from the cetaceans from Eric, who kindly allowed me to use them, which expand on the information given to me by the whale sharks and giant mantas.

www.peaceinthewater.com
Peace in the Water is a global movement bringing into reality the vision of peace and protection for dolphins, whales and all marine life.

radicaljoyforhardtimes.org
Radical Joy for Hard Times reconciles people and wounded places through compassion, curiosity, and acts of beauty, so no part of the earth is orphaned from the cycle of life. We believe that creating a sustainable, equitable, thriving future on Earth depends upon opening our hearts to the natural world.

www.whitelions.org
The Global White Lion Protection Trust is a non-profit conservation and community development organisation, established in 2002 by author and conservationist, Linda Tucker.

www.lionrescue.org.za
Drakenstein Lion Park, a sanctuary for captive born lions.

www.baboonmatters.org.za
Baboon Matters, dedicated to the rescue and rehabilitation of baboons in need.

www.wildoceanadventures.com
providing once in a lifetime opportunities to encounter some of the most amazing and intelligent animals on the planet.

www.shambhala.co.uk
Shambhala Healing Retreat, Glastonbury. Sacred journeys to Egypt run by Isis "Visionary, Teacher of Healers, Facilitator of Egyptian Initiations, Bringer of Joy, Lover of Life".

www.k1photography.com
Wildlife photographer Karen-Jane Dudley.

www.mcsuk.org
Marine Conservation Society.

www.sharktrust.org
Shark Trust. UK charity for shark conservation.

www.ecohealthalliance.org
Eco Health Alliance, formally the Wildlife Trust.

BIBLIOGRAPHY

Baumann Brunke, Dawn *Animal Voices*   Inner Traditions, 2002

Broadhurst, Paul and Miller, Hamish *The Sun and the Serpent*   Pendragon Press, 1989

Emoto, Masaru *The True Power of Water: Healing and Discovering Ourselves*
   Beyond Words Pub., 2005

Haliwell, Tanis *Summer with Leprechauns*   Blue Dolphin, 1997

Holly, Thea *Listening to Trees*   Capall Bann Publishing, 2001

Hope, Murry *The Sirius Connection*   Element Books, 1996

Hope, Murry *The Lion People: Intercosmic Messages from the Future*   Thoth, 1988

Mehler, Stephen S. *Land of Osiris*   Adventures Unlimited Press, 2002

Melchizedek, Drunvalo *Serpent of Light Beyond 2012*   Weiser, 2008

Smedley, Jenny *Pets Have Souls Too*   Hay House Inc., 2009

Tucker, Linda *Mystery of the White Lions: Children of the Sun God*   Hay House Inc., 2010

Villoldo, Alberto *Mending the Past and Healing the Future with Soul Retrieval*
   Hay House, 2006

Walker, Madeleine *An Exchange of Love: Animals Healing People in Past, Present and Future Lifetimes*
   O Books, 2009

ABOUT THE AUTHOR

Madeleine Walker works as horse and rider trauma consultant, empowerment coach and healer. She runs clinics and individual sessions with animals and their human carers. She has become a recognized expert on past life connections between animals and their owners and the way unresolved issues can affect current life problems, from emotional and physical challenges, to relationships. Her work as an empowerment coach has facilitated wonderful results with her human clients.

She is also now one of the world's leading animal intuitives. She has written the 'Paws for Thought' column for Vision Magazine and currently writes a column for Holistic Healing@about.com, an online magazine. She also performs distant readings for clients internationally and facilitates courses and workshops both in the UK and abroad. She travels extensively to work with species in the wild and will be leading groups to experience profound encounters with cetaceans and white lions in the near future. Her workshop 'Gateways to the Ancients' offers profound reconnection to Cetacean, Atlantian, Ancient Egyptian, Shamanic Elders, and Outer Planetary energies. She is a consultant for spiritual forums on animal communication and healing. She also works alongside holistic veterinary surgeons. She has been featured in *Kindred Spirit, Chat its Fate, Prediction, Fate and Fortune,* and *Rainbow News* in New Zealand and has also been a guest on many radio shows in the UK, Canada, USA and Australia. She has been featured on an Animal World documentary with Suprememaster TV, translated into many different languages and shown globally on Satellite TV. Madeleine lives with her son Cameron and their animals in Somerset.

Her website is: www.anexchangeoflove.com

"Madeleine is one of the most sensitive and accurate
animal psychics in the world."
—Carolyn Burdet, former editor of *Kindred Spirit*

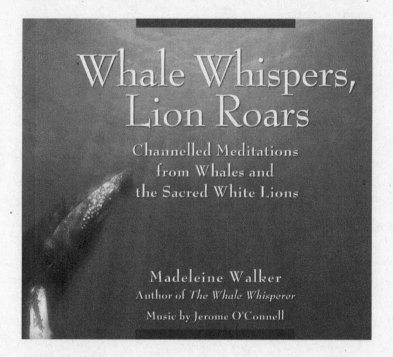

Whale Whispers,
Lion Roars

Channelled Meditations
from Whales and
the Sacred White Lions

Madeleine Walker
Author of *The Whale Whisperer*
Music by Jerome O'Connell

This CD is the companion to *The Whale Whisperer*.
Accompanied by human musicians, the meditations
on this CD were channelled from the animals who wish
to re-empower us in order for us to step up to the
plate and start saving mother earth!

ISBN 978-1-84409-541-4

Available from your local bookseller,
or directly from publisher: www.findhornpress.com

FINDHORN PRESS

Life-Changing Books

Consult our catalogue online
(with secure order facility) on
www.findhornpress.com

For information on the Findhorn Foundation:
www.findhorn.org